WHEN BABY BOOM WOMEN RETIRE

WHEN BABY BOOM WOMEN RETIRE

CR

Nancy Dailey

Westport, Connecticut
London

Library of Congress Cataloging-in-Publication Data

Dailey, Nancy, 1953–
    When baby boom women retire / Nancy Dailey.
        p. cm.
    Includes bibliographical references and index.
    ISBN 0–275–96070–6 (alk. paper)
    1. Women—United States—Retirement. 2. Baby boom generation—
United States—Retirement. 3. Retirement income—United States.
I. Title.
HQ1063.2.U6D35 1998
306.3'8'082—dc21   97–27003

British Library Cataloguing in Publication Data is available.

Library of Congress Catalog Card Number: 97–27003
ISBN: 0–275–96070–6

First published in 1998

Praeger Publishers, 88 Post Road West, Westport, CT 06881
An imprint of Greenwood Publishing Group, Inc.

Printed in the United States of America

The paper used in this book complies with the
Permanent Paper Standard issued by the National
Information Standards Organization (Z39.48–1984).

10 9 8 7 6 5 4 3

Contents

Illustrations

TABLES

FIGURES

Preface

Fewer than 20% of baby boom women can feel secure about their future retirement. Baby boom women who are married, possess a college degree, receive high earnings, and own a home can expect to experience a comfortable retirement. Yet, even these women may face economic jeopardy since risk factors such as divorce or loss of a job could reduce their future prospects. Marriage, education, occupation and home ownership—these are the variables that best predict the future for baby boom women. Possession of all four variables indicate high retirement security; absence of any one of the variables increases the risk of poverty in old age.

This study reports on an in-depth examination of three key structural variables impacting the future retirement of baby boom women: population aging, baby boom women's labor force participation, and retirement income sources. The study's findings reveal: (1) that baby boom women's retirement will not look like men's retirement patterns; (2) that traditional sources of retirement income—Social Security, employer pensions and personal savings—for most baby boom women will be insufficient; and (3) that baby boom women will enter retirement as society's caregivers of the country's elderly.

Acknowledgments

I first need to thank my husband, Patrick Shields, and my business partner, Kelly O'Brien, both fellow baby boomers, for their support and encouragement. I would also like to acknowledge Dr. Jurg Siegenthaler, sociology professor at The American University in Washington, D.C. for his assistance and encouragement throughout the development of this study.

1

The Baby Boom
and the Right to Retire

INTRODUCTION

Have baby boom women "earned" the right to retirement? What will the retirement experience be for "baby boom" women, those cohort groups born between 1946–1964 who will begin to retire around 2010? Will there be "retirement," as we now know it, for the women of the baby boom generation? Using the existing definitions and parameters of retirement, the overwhelming majority of baby boom women will not have earned the right to retire in spite of spending almost thirty years in the paid labor force. This book identifies and isolates the variables that are the true predictors of the retirement experience for baby boom women.

Baby boom women will not replicate the retirement experience of their mothers, nor will their retirement experience look like men's retirement. Life in retirement for baby boom women will be fundamentally different from their mothers' experience and from that of their male counterparts. Current assumptions about work and retirement in our capitalist economy may not be valid for women. The history of work and retirement is really the story of men's work and retirement. Women's retirement had been virtually ignored until the 1980s (Calasanti, 1993). Our current structure of retirement was built on the male work experience; it assumes a "traditional" nuclear family that consists of a lifelong breadwinner. Within this structure, women's retirement is dependent on the retirement income gained from men. A clear distinction between men and women's retirement experience is the greater dependence of women, whether married or widowed, on the earnings of their spouse (Holden & Smeeding, 1990).

Over the past thirty years, while many men and their spouses have benefited from this retirement model, the nature of work has changed significantly. The dramatic increase of women in the labor force, changing family patterns, and the restructuring of the economy will impact the retirement of the baby boom cohort groups. It is not even clear whether the current retirement model will serve baby boom men well, let alone baby boom women.

Labor statistics show that women are beginning to exhibit life time labor force participation patterns similar to those of men and that men are working fewer full-time years (U.S. Department of Labor, 1994). Popular assumptions and predictions have taken the "appearance" of these statistics and concluded that what has worked for men will also work for women. However, it is not safe to assume that women's retirement decisions, options and experience will follow the pattern of previous generations of men.

The new economic reality, coupled with the population aging of the United States, will intersect with the life choices and decisions of baby boom women to create their retirement destiny. Throughout the 20th century, women's retirement has existed as a subset of men's retirement. Baby boom women will be the first generation of women to have the option of defining their own retirement. They are the first female cohort whose labor force participation will span most of their adult life. The intent of this book is to sort myth from fact, in an effort to discern what this cohort can really expect in their old age.

In order to investigate the retirement experience of baby boom women, the material base and social status of these women will be examined through the use of empirical data or "appearances." This method of inquiry will clarify the structures that affect baby boom women and generate data to predict and forecast their retirement experience. Social structures (even retirement, which has a relatively brief history compared to other institutions) become entrenched within society, and tend to be relatively stable. Social Security is a primary example, with its stable definitions of entitlement and structure of payout. It is therefore assumed here that the basic structure of retirement will remain the same with little expectation of structural changes to accommodate women's retirement needs. To substantiate this position, the social relations and structures that will determine the retirement experience, options and decisions for baby boom women are examined. "Appearances" are scrutinized to assess the social condition of baby boom women and to reveal the variables that will influence the outcome of their retirement opportunities. Reliance on observable facts alone often leads to superficial and overly ideological conclusions. Going beyond appearances will unmask the true nature of retirement for baby boom women.

Institutional inertia often perpetuates overreliance on observable facts or appearances, leading to false assumptions about the true nature of a structure. For this reason, an in-depth examination of empirical data relating to three structural variables—population aging, labor force participation, and retirement income sources—is made. The search revealed several implicit assumptions about baby boom women and baby boom retirement:

• Assumption #1: Women's retirement will resemble men's retirement since their labor force patterns look similar.

• Assumption #2: The traditional three-legged stool of retirement income—Social Security, employer pensions and personal savings—will continue to finance baby boom retirement. The retirement blueprint used for their parents will suffice for the baby boom.

• Assumption #3: Women will continue as society's caregivers regardless of their labor force participation. The difference for baby boom women will be the extension of this care from children to the elderly.

These assumptions maintain and promote existing retirement structures. Taken at face value or solely on "appearance," they lead to a set of conclusions about the future of retirement for baby boom women that may not expose the true nature of work and retirement for women. The following chapters reveal the validity of these assumptions by researching: (1) how retirement is studied; (2) how shifts in population aging will impact women's retirement; (3) how the nature of work determines retirement income; and (4) how baby boom women's life choices will create their retirement destiny. This study exposes and interprets existing population, labor force and income data and offers insight into what the future holds for baby boom women.

The research questions that will be answered in this book are:

1. What will the impact be of demographic changes and population aging on the retirement experience of women? What role do baby boom women play in population aging and will their destiny be determined by their demographics?

2. Will a retirement population, like the baby boom cohort group, growing in relative size, place an insupportable burden on workers resulting in the delay

of retirement or an increase in employment of older workers, in particular, older women workers?

3. How will the nature of work in a post-industrial capitalist economy impact the retirement of baby boom women? Will women retire as soon as it is financially feasible? Or, will retirement elude baby boom women as demographic pressures grow in an aging America?

4. What will be the sources of retirement income for baby boom women?

5. How do age and gender, as structural features of social relations, impact the employability of older women? How does (and will) this impact their retirement experience?

6. Will there be one future or several futures for baby boom women?

A LOOK AT THE BABY BOOM GENERATION

In the 1970s, the phrase "baby boom generation" began to be used to describe the biggest fertility splurge in the history of the United States, reversing a century-long decline in the fertility rate. Credit for popularizing the phrase has been given to Landon Jones, who coined it in his book, *Great Expectations: America & the Baby Boom Generation* (American Demographics, 1993a). The phrase is now widely used and refers to about 76 million Americans, comprising one third of the total U.S. population (see Table 1).

No single theory exists to explain the baby boom, and debate continues about the reasons for this fertility binge. However, most experts agree that it was a combination of cultural, social and economic factors. Russell (1982) attributes the primary demographic causes of the baby boom to the following:

• More women married than ever before.

• More women who married had children.

• Women had their children earlier.

• And some women had more children.

Only a minor part of the baby boom can be attributed to increases in the proportion of women having three or more births (Westoff, 1978). The proportion of women having five or more children actually declined among mothers of baby boomers. The baby boom was not a return to the 19th century family. Demographers agree that the fundamental reason was the increase in the number of women having at least two children. This number increased by 50% between the 1930s and the 1950s (Light, 1988).

The theoretical explanations for why the mothers of baby boomers moved away from spinsterhood, childless marriage and the one-child family and toward early marriage, early childbirth and the two-child family center on the cultural, social and economic conditions faced by the "Depression" cohort group of the late 1920s and 1930s. Easterlin's theory of relative cohort size emphasizes economic factors while the work of other authors such as Jones, Light and Russell highlight cultural and social changes. Bouvier and DeVita (1991) summarize the prevailing literature regarding the rush into marriage and parenting and identify the following causal factors:

• The U.S. economy was expanding rapidly after World War II.

• The GI Bill for education and Veterans Administration loans made secondary education and housing more attainable.

• Demand for labor was strong and men's wages were rising, putting little economic pressure on women to enter the paid labor force.

• There was a resurgence of traditional family values with the husband as breadwinner and the wife as homeworker.

• An ambivalence toward birth control by couples, combined with young mothers facing many years of being exposed to the risk of an unwanted pregnancy contributed to the surge in births.

The convergence of these causal factors resulted in a nineteen year period (see Table 1), 1946–1964, of unprecedented fertility, roughly 3.8 million births per year in the early years of the boom, 4.6 million per year in the peak years, and 4.3 million per year in the final years (Kingson, 1992).

The baby boom is often defined in monolithic terms, producing misleading generalizations that are frequently popularized in the mass media. The only generalizations which can accurately be made about the baby boom, as a cohort group, is that it possesses two enduring characteristics: (1) its size; and (2) its diversity. Although considered a "generation," baby boomers are more disparate than similar. Diversity in demographic variables such as education, occupation, marriage, divorce, race, gender, ethnicity, religion, even geographic region, illustrates the complexity of this cohort group.

Researchers commonly split the baby boom into two age groups—early boomers and later boomers. Early boomers (leading edge) were born from 1946–1954; later boomers (trailing edge) from 1955–1964. The leading edge of the baby boom was at the vanguard for change and have enjoyed more advantages than their younger siblings. The trailing edge of the baby boom are more numerous and face more competition. Differences in educational attainment, income, home ownership and rates of poverty can now be seen between the leading and trailing edge boomers. For example, educational attainment (to the college level) of the late boomers has been significantly less than that achieved by the early boomers (i.e., only one-fourth of trailing edge men have graduated from college, while one-third of leading edge men have). As Figure 1 illustrates, just about every group follows this trend. The reverse may be likely for later female baby boomers as they continue to narrow the educational gap between their older sisters and male boomers. In general, this lower educational attainment is accompanied by lower income and lower rates of home ownership as well as by higher rates of poverty.

Table 1
Number of Baby Boomers, 1950–1990 (in Thousands)

Age Group	Year				
	1950	1960	1970	1980	1990
0–4	16,614	20,231			
5–9		18,692	16,174		
10–14		16,773	20,789		
15–19			19,070	17,151	
20–24			16,371	21,293	
25–29				19,471	17,434
30–34				17,710	22,414
35–39					20,220
40–44					17,677
Total	16,614	55,696	72,404	75,625	77,745
Median Age	2	7	15	25	35
Baby Boomers as a % of Total Population	10.8%	30.4%	34.8%	33.4%	31.0%

Source: Adapted from "Aging Baby Boomers: How Secure Is Their Economic Future?" *American Association of Retired Persons*. Washington, D.C.: 1994. Pamphlet.

There is concern that late boomers may be at greater risk in old age if these trends continue, especially since it may be compounded by the racial and ethnic diversity of the baby boom.

As the baby boom ages, its cultural and economic diversity is becoming increasingly apparent. This diversity makes forecasting future retirement scenarios for the baby boom a complex endeavor, especially for baby boom women. Consideration needs to be given to gender differences among the baby boom as well as the variations among baby boom women themselves (i.e., occupation, education, race, etc.). Chapter 4, "The Changing Nature of Work and Its Impact on Baby Boom Women's Retirement," and Chapter 5, "Retirement Income for Women," will examine these differences in depth.

Figure 1
Early Boomers Better Educated (March 1991 CPS)

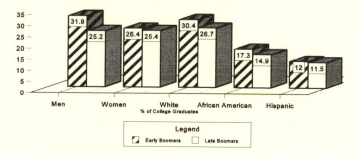

Source: Adapted from *Aging Baby Boomers: How Secure Is Their Economic Future?* American Association of Retired Persons, Washington, D.C.: 1994. Pamphlet.

The baby boom's size and diversity will ensure that their retirement will be very different from that of its parents. Baby boomers, on the whole, grew up with parents whose financial status improved steadily each year. As children and adolescents, baby boomers were better housed, fed, clothed, and educated than any previous generation. As adults, babyboomers watched as their parents and grandparents moved into retirement at earlier and earlier ages with a sense of entitlement or the "right" to retirement. Although retirement as a social institution is relatively new, the notion of an "earned" retirement has become firmly entrenched in American society.

Baby boomers entered the labor force adopting this normative expectation. However, the institutional mechanisms (Social Security, long-term employment, pensions, Medicare, Medicaid), which run the retirement machine for their parents, have been influenced by many uncertainties and risks that are now challenging the future level and adequacy of retirement living for baby boomers. Some of the uncertainties and risks that will affect the well-being of baby boomers in retirement are: (1) their own demographic and economic characteristics; (2) the health of the economy; (3) the ability of social and political institutions to adapt to changes in the population structure; (4) the risks of inflation on savings; (5) the varieties of private pension coverage among industries and occupations, and the influence of job change or loss on pension rights; and (6) the ultimate level of Social Security benefits—which are deeply impacted when individuals are out of the regular labor force for long periods of time due to structural unemployment, illness or child care obligations. This last point is particularly pertinent to baby boom women and will be discussed in the following chapters.

Ironically, even in light of these uncertainties and risks, many working baby boomers feel confident they will have a secure retirement. A 1994 EBRI/Greenwald Retirement Confidence Survey reported that 66% of working Americans aged 26 and over were "very" (21%) or "somewhat" (45%) confident about their financial security in retirement. Perhaps one reason for this confidence stems from the fact that current workers are beginning to save for retirement at a younger age than current retirees did. The survey reports that current workers started saving for retirement, on average, at age 30 compared to age 38 for current retirees. Early savings behavior may be providing baby boomers an illusion of security given the other demographic and economic handicaps they may be facing. In addition, a 1993 survey conducted by Merrill Lynch & Co. indicated that women are more likely to postpone savings for retirement than their male counterparts due to more immediate savings needs such as children's education, and purchase of a car or house. This does not bode well for baby boom women if they are postponing retirement savings or if they are adopting a false sense of security about their retirement future.

What can baby boomers really expect from their retirement years? Two theoretical positions dominate the literature about the future of retirement in the United States—the intergenerational crisis perspective and the gradual adjustment perspective (Kingson & O'Grady-LeShane, 1991). The first perspective suggests that the size of the baby boom itself will overwhelm public mechanisms and precipitate intergenerational strife. The intergenerational crisis perspective fundamentally debates the role of government in a market economy. The "doomsayers of Social Security" are often found in this debate, forecasting a very unpleasant retirement for the baby boom. The second view, the gradual adjustment perspective, while acknowledging the obstacles to a secure retirement, suggests that these obstacles can be overcome by gradual adjustments in existing retirement and health policies and programs. This position fundamentally argues that problems will be solved incrementally in a less rational, comprehensive manner. It assumes that existing policies and programs (e.g., Social Security) will adapt over time to changing social, political and economic conditions (Kingson & O'Grady-LeShane, 1991). These two perspectives offer contrasting forecasts: (1) a very pessimistic outlook—one that is dark, plagued by economic stagnation, inter-generational conflict and the erosion of family care-giving networks; or (2) a cautiously optimistic prospect—one that is promising, dominated by economic growth and intergenerational compassion.

If one ascribes to Easterlin's theory that "demography is destiny," the baby boom's retirement will be dominated by its demographics. As baby boomers move into retirement they will be the "bearers of structure" creating retirement in their own likeness. Landon Jones (1980) postulates in his book, *Great Expectations*, that one of the ideas that binds the baby boom as a generation, regardless of their diversity, is the belief that they have a mission in life. As they grow older, will their mission in life be to secure their retirement by making the gradual adjustments necessary for a viable retirement or will they reinvent it by demanding substantial systemic changes in the structure of retirement? This is an especially provocative question for baby boom women since they will live far longer in retirement, with less income, than their male counterparts.

Its shear size, its position within the population structure (between two substantially smaller generations) and its diversity make the baby boom generation a reckoning force for demographers, social scientists, politicians, policy-makers, economists, business analysts, etc. The baby boom dominates the demographics of the United States and will continue to do so. As this critical mass moves through its life cycle, it has and will change our social institutions—education, work, marriage, and family. As it approaches middle and old age it will alter, one way or another, the institution of retirement. As a group, baby boomers tended to invest in education, enter the labor force later, marry later in life, end marriages more frequently, delay childbearing, and have fewer children. Baby boomers have postponed entry into various phases of the life cycle and it would appear that they will continue this pattern with retirement. The demographic, economic, and political implications of retirement for the baby boom generation is of great social concern. With the retirement of the baby boom generation, the United States will face the longest period of retirement for the largest and best educated generation in our history. The significance of examining the retirement experience of baby boom women is:

1. very little study has been given to the retirement experience of women, past, present or future; although the study of baby boom retirement has increased, especially as the cohort group moves through middle age, little or no focus has been given to the future state of women's retirement;

2. the substantial growth in the labor force participation rate of women makes the study of the retirement of women increasingly important;

3. the demographic changes in the U.S. population make aging a women's issue that will heavily influence the institution of retirement;

4. the economic future for women retirees is unclear; however, it is clear that they will likely encounter many more financial obstacles than men; and

5. the polarity in the debate about the future of retirement hinders women's retirement planning and preparation; baby boom retirement will most likely occur somewhere between the "doomsayers" scenario and the "bright future" scenario, and more clarity is needed to help women prepare for their future.

The baby boom spent its youth during one of the longest periods of sustained economic growth in U.S. history. It will spend its aging during a period of tremendous economic uncertainty and transition. The promise of retirement security may be an illusion for many baby boom women. Taken at face value ("appearance"), America's retirement system is non-discriminatory or gender-neutral. However, despite making greater contributions to the paid labor force than any other female cohort group, the majority of working women today (baby boomers) do not have access to a private pension plan, and those who do will be significantly penalized by the way the employer-sponsored pension system interacts with women's work patterns (U.S. House Select Committee on Aging, 1992). Given the complex social and financial challenges baby boom women will face, it is critical that women, first, become informed about what they can expect in their old age and, secondly, act on their own behalf to secure their retirement. The 1993 Merrill Lynch survey reported that twice as many female (35%) as male (17%) baby boomers said they felt uninformed about their retirement benefits. More women than men, in general, said they would rather have someone else manage their retirement investments (Bernheim, 1993). This apparent reticence about retirement planning needs to be confronted if baby boom women want some control over their retirement destiny.

The social forces of aging also make the study of the retirement experience of baby boom women significant. The difference in life span between men and women, the sheer numbers of the baby boom generation, the future of caregiving for the elderly, the labor force participation of women entitling them to Social Security income, all make this topic imperative to understand and forecast. Currently, women over the age of 75 outnumber men two to one; aging, retirement and old age are clearly issues about and for women. Gender, as well as social class and other structural variables, is a major factor in understanding trends in retirement. Gender, aging and the "right" to retirement are all variables that will shape the retirement experience of the baby boom generation (Schulz, 1992).

Finally, the prevailing paradigm within which retirement is viewed is insufficient to predict or project what retirement will be or mean to baby boom women. Traditional or undifferentiated analytical approaches cannot be utilized, because of the diversity of their demographic variables—education, occupation, marriage, divorce, gender, race, income, and life expectancy. A search beyond empirical appearances will provide a more revealing and accurate picture of the future retirement model for baby boom women. The current, male-dominated model is based on a linear design which assumes a simple cause-and-effect relationship between work and retirement. For the baby boomers, especially women, there is no reliable blueprint for retirement. There is need for an heuristic device to address the complexity of the processes that will determine the retirement experience for baby boom women. A shift in how retirement is studied, analyzed and perceived is necessary to reasonably determine what that model will look like, because, just as baby boom women have changed the landscape of the work force, they will also change the institution of retirement.

The logical path of inquiry for studying the future retirement of baby boom women is a relatively deductive process beginning with an examination of the influence of population aging on baby boom women's behavior as a cohort group. This is followed by an analysis of the nature of work for baby boom women, which sets the parameters for viewing their sources of income in retirement. This flow of inquiry uses the filter of baby boom women to scrutinize data regarding population aging, labor force participation and retirement income. While this book may generate more questions than answers, it will hopefully contribute to the development of theoretical constructs. It may help guide future researchers to formulate more accurate assumptions, data collection methods and analytical practices of women's work and retirement behavior.

2

The Status of Women
in the Retirement Literature

This chapter provides a short review of the study's methodology, followed by an examination of the status of women in the retirement literature. A brief introduction of retirement as a social institution and how it is analyzed and studied will help explain the status of research on women's retirement. A discussion of methodological issues will highlight problems related to the study of women's retirement. Finally, prospects for the study of baby boom women's retirement experience will also be explored.

METHODOLOGY AND DATA

The somewhat chaotic condition of current retirement research helps explain the many methodological and data problems encountered in the study of women's retirement. This study is an effort to find order among the chaos by examining existing empirical data about baby boom women which clarify the variables that influence women's retirement. While much has been done on the topic of retirement, there has been little study of baby boom retirement issues and virtually no study of baby boom women's retirement.

The group under study is "baby boom" women; women born between 1946–1964. Secondary data sources such as census data, unpublished tabulations and statistics from the Bureau of Labor Statistics (BLS) taken from the 1990 Current Population Survey, prominent retirement studies, and literature on working women will be the foundation for inquiry. Data will be examined, analyzed and evaluated within the framework of the research questions. Methods of data sharing, such as tables, charts, and figures that present quantitative data are patterned and adapted after those found in the literature (e.g., BLS' labor force statistics, Statistical Handbook, U.S. Bureau of the Census reports, etc.). Data are organized and presented using standard formats, for example, labor force participation rates are presented in the manner used by the Bureau of Labor Statistics, albeit with data specific to baby boom women. Data manipulated to generate statistics specific to baby boom women and men follow standard calculation and reporting methods.

Measures

The year 1990 is the benchmark year from which baby boom women will be analyzed. Current Population Survey data, population data and Bureau of Labor Statistics reporting procedures dictate how statistics are measured and described. The year 1990 is the first interval when all baby boom women fit into two discreet age groups: 25–34 years of age (later boomers) and 35–44 years of age (early boomers). The "baby boom" is a nineteen-year time period and, therefore, does not fit precisely into existing reporting categories. Data are collected and reported in ten-year increments. It is not possible to extract those born in 1965 from the tabulations from secondary data sources, but the inclusion of this year (1965) should have no sway in the overall data interpretations since the objective of this study is to search for patterns or trends.

Procedure

The focus of this study is to provide an in-depth analysis of existing empirical data, revealing the true nature of work and retirement for baby boom women. The analytical approach used to sort "appearance" from fact will be:

1. an examination of selected structural variables using existing methods and standard interpretive guidelines;

2. the isolation of baby boom women's behavior within each of the structural variables (i.e., fertility behavior, labor force participation rates, etc.); and

3. the comparison and contrasting of baby boom women with other female cohort groups and with baby boom men.

Published statistics measuring population demographics, labor force participation, occupation and industry statistics, retirement patterns for women, pension coverage, asset income, employment income, and Social Security income are examined. Qualitative data collected from the literature on aging, work, women's employment and income and retirement are also utilized. Analysis of trends, comparison of patterns and examination of assumptions underlying projections about baby boom retirement are made. The intent of this approach is to differentiate "appearance" from fact, allowing for a more accurate picture of the future of retirement for baby boom women.

An examination of studies relating to retirement will be made but will be limited to studies that make projections about the future of retirement and, in particular, the retirement experience of women. For example, a 1992 report from the Subcommittee on Retirement Income from the U.S. House Select Committee on Aging shows that during old age, the risk of being poor is 70% greater for a woman than it is for a man. Analysis and interpretation for relevancy to baby boom women's life and work experience will be made with current reports. As is noted further in this chapter, generational assumptions are inherent in all reports on retirement and may not always be applicable to baby boom women.

The methodology employed in this study allows insight into what the structure of retirement may be for baby boom women. Data generated to answer the research questions are compared and contrasted with current women's retirement, thereby helping to formulate possible future retirement scenarios for baby boom women. Methods and procedures used to examine the research questions include:

1. A review of the literature on the economic impact of future population changes in advanced industrial countries. The work done by Easterlin and the Committee for Economic Development is utilized as well as data analysis from the Statistical Abstract and Current Population Survey reports.

2. An evaluation of baby boom women's current and projected labor force participation rates as well as an analysis of where women work—the types of work, occupations and industries. Comparisons to the labor force participation rates of baby boom men and other female cohort groups are made. Unpublished 1990 tabulations and statistics from the Bureau of Labor Statistics (BLS) taken from the 1990 Current Population Survey are the basis of analysis of baby boom women and men. Use of unpublished data was necessary since all other secondary data sources provide only summary information by age and sex. Assistance from experienced BLS staff members, Diane Herz and Thomas Nardone, both economists at the Washington, D.C., offices was solicited.

3. An assessment of current and future women's employment income, pension coverage, asset income and Social Security income. Data and data analysis

from sources such as the *Social Security Bulletin and Monthly Labor Review*, gerontological journals, pension trade journals (i.e., Journal of the American Society of CLU & ChFC), and the Pension Rights Center are employed.

Synthesis and summary of the data and information revealed in the process of answering the research questions lead to a hypothesis about the retirement future of baby boom women. It also substantiates the main thesis of this book: Baby boom women will not replicate the retirement experience of their mothers, nor will their retirement experience look like men's retirement. Gender and age biases within the structures of work and retirement will ensure that baby boom women's retirement will be very different from that of their mothers and their male counterparts.

THE STATUS OF WOMEN IN THE RETIREMENT LITERATURE

Retirement is a phenomenon of modern industrial society; an artifact of the Industrial Revolution. The early development of retirement was very much influenced by industrialization, the union movement, serious problems in the economy and the negative views of the productive capacity of older workers. The inception of the Social Security program made retirement come of age (Atchley, 1988). As the idea of retirement has continued to mature during the shifts in the U.S. economy, it has come to embody the idea that by virtue of a long-term contribution (market labor) to the growth and prosperity of society, its individual members earn the right to a share of the nation's prosperity in their later years without paid employment (Schulz, 1992). This sense of entitlement embraced by American workers has facilitated the short, but impressive, history of this social institution. The notion of retirement has ingrained itself into our social fabric with remarkable speed. The twentieth century saw this institution embed itself into the social structure, redefining the social role of the elderly population while instilling expectations of leisure in old age for the American worker. Most adults expect to retire and most of them expect to retire before age 65. All evidence indicates that most workers, men and women, retire as soon as it is financially feasible.

Overall, labor force participation tends to be high until age 50 when it begins to gradually decline. There is a significant drop in participation at age 62 and again at age 65 corresponding to the age of first eligibility for Social Security retirement benefits and the age of eligibility for "full" benefits. Although there has been much discussion in the retirement literature on the continuing trend toward early retirement, the median retirement age continues to hover at 62 years of age for both men and women (Table 2).

Table 2
Median Age at Retirement, by Sex, 1950–1955 to 2000–2005

Year	Age	
	Men	Women
1950–55	66.9	67.7
1955–60	65.8	66.2
1960–65	65.2	64.6
1965–70	64.2	64.2
1970–75	63.4	63.0
1975–80	63.0	63.2
1980–85	62.8	62.7
1985–90	62.6	62.8
1990–95[1]	62.7	62.6
1995–2000[2]	62.3	62.0
2000–05[3]	61.7	61.2

[1]Based on 1990 actual and 1995 projected data.
[2]Based on projected data for 1995 and 2000.
[3]Based on projected data for 2000 and 2005
Note: Estimates were calculated from 5-year age-specific labor force data obtained in the Current Population Survey and life-table survival ratios.

Source: Gendell, Murray and J.S. Siegel. "Trends in Retirement Age by Sex, 1950–2005." *Monthly Labor Review* (July, 1992): 22–29.

During the second half of this century, the combination of two social changes—early retirement and increased longevity—reshaped the retirement experience. The net effect has been a significant expansion of both the number of years and the proportion of Americans' life-spans spent in retirement. In 1940, the average man spent about nine years, 15% of his life span in retirement. By 1990, the average man spent nearly fourteen years, or more than one fifth of his life-span in retirement (U.S. House Select Committee on Aging, 1992).

The Retirement Literature

Retirement now plays a considerable role in the life course of Americans and subsequently has drawn an increasing interest of social scientists. To date, the overwhelming pursuit in the study of retirement has been the economic and financial outcomes and implications of retirement decision-making processes. The literature is dominated by studies of retirement timing, attitudes toward retirement and pre-retirement planning. The intent of most of these studies appears to be: (1) to help shape and set policy for the administration of Social Security; (2) to advise in financial planning for pension funds; and (3) to guide social policy relating to the elderly portion of the dependent population. Very little of the study of retirement has been dedicated to the development of theory—to help forecast and predict the retirement behavior or experience of future generations or cohort groups such as baby boom women. This lack of a strong theoretical basis has led to an overreliance on economic and statistical modeling—a practice that gives little attention to the impact of other factors in the retirement process (Leonesio, 1993). The dominant ideology surrounding the study of retirement has created several methodological predicaments. Serious flaws in the structure of analysis and data reliability have created obstacles that challenge the ability of researchers to study retirement in new and different ways.

Existing research of retirement suffers from a methodological quandary—the lack of an appropriate and accurate definition of retirement. This analytical dilemma for researchers is becoming more pronounced as interest in women's retirement increases. Recent work on women's retirement has revealed, more clearly than ever, that throughout the retirement literature, the concept of retirement is defined inconsistently for both men and women (Slevin & Wingrove, 1995; Talaga & Beehr, 1995; Weaver, 1994; Calasanti, 1993; Leonesio, 1993; Szinovacz & Washo, 1992; Hayward & Grady, 1990; Palmore, et al., 1985). For women the tremendous variability of their work histories compounds the issue of definition (Belgrave, 1989; Fox, 1977). Definition drives operationalization; how retirement is defined and operationalized creates the relationship between certain predictors (e.g., health, financial status, occupational level, marital status, etc.) and retirement (Talaga & Beehr, 1995). Prevailing studies frequently use both objective (i.e., receiving a pension, working less than full-time, etc.) and subjective criteria (i.e., self-attribution, respondent's assessment of his/her retirement status, etc.) to define retirement (Perkins, 1993; Gendell and Siegal, 1992). The lack of one best way to measure retirement has created the practice of multiple operationalizations—the use of objective and subjective criteria within a single study. The problem of definition is most apparent when findings from one retirement study are compared with those of another study, often with little regard given to the exact definition of retirement being used (Talaga & Beehr, 1995; Leonesio, 1993). It has led to conflicting conclusions about the importance of predictors and causal factors when in reality it is likely that no two studies are examining the same phenomenon. This practice raises serious methodological questions about replicability, reliability and validity.

The difficulty in definition and operationalization can be attributed to the nature of retirement itself. Retirement is both a status and a process, hence the inclination to utilize both objective and subjective criteria. The traditional and popular notion of retirement as a single, isolated event that ends a person's labor force participation is woefully inadequate to describe and analyze the condition of retirement (Szinovacz & Washo, 1992; Hayward & Grady, 1990). Retirement involves the intersection of social and economic factors, on both the micro and macro levels. It is a complex process that must account for individual work life circumstances as well as important life events such as changes in marital status or illness or death while incorporating macro level influences such as economic and social conditions, and social policy.

While inconsistencies exist throughout the retirement literature, there have been constant patterns of study. Past research has consistently studied retirement: (1) through the ideological lens of white men; and (2) as an event—withdrawal from the labor market (Slevin & Wingrove, 1995; Calasanti, 1993; Szinovacz & Washo, 1992; Erdner and Guy, 1990; Wise, 1990). The study of retirement has centered on the male experience, treating it as the single act of departing from market labor. This double bias is persistently represented throughout the literature with most empirical retirement studies concentrating on white male wage and salary workers (Leonesio, 1993; Szinovacz & Washo, 1992). Doeringer (1990) suggests that in recent years there has been movement away from viewing retirement as a discrete event toward viewing it as an interdependent process hinging on life events and decisions. To date, this theoretical shift has been slow to impact retirement studies reported in the literature.

The wide range of studies that do exist on retirement most frequently use the following objective and subjective criteria to define retirement: (1) the receipt of a pension, whether public or private; (2) permanent withdrawal from the labor force at some advanced age for reasons other than death; and (3) identification as being retired (Leonesio, 1993; Perkins, 1993; Gendell & Siegel, 1992; Ekerdt & DeViney, 1990). Talaga and Beehr (1995) indicate in their analysis of the literature that the collective research essentially uses four broad areas of measurement:

- retirees tend to be older, usually over the age of at least 50 years;

- retirees tend to spend less of their time working for pay;

- retirees are more likely to receive some income that is specifically designated for retirees (e.g., private pensions, Social Security);

- retirees tend to think of themselves as being retired.

These criteria are general in nature and less exact but reflect an inclusive sense of retirement. The search for how and when people retire has led researchers to use a variety of predictors (e.g., presence of dependents in the household, occupational level, spouse's health, financial and employment status, etc.). These predictors vary somewhat within studies and vary greatly across studies. Many supposedly objective measures of retirement (e.g., not working full-time all year, eligibility for pensions or Social Security) are problematic for women because of the diversity of female work histories (Hatch & Thompson, 1992b; Palmore, et al., 1985; Fox, 1977). The most obvious predictor, age, appears to be the strongest theoretical predictor for both men and women (Talaga & Beehr, 1995). However, age alone is insufficient to predict current and future work or retirement behavior. Overreliance on age as a predictor is especially troublesome for women since age masks the true variables that impact women's work and retirement behavior (see Chapter 4, "The Changing Nature of Work and Its Impact on Baby Boom Women's Retirement").

An echo throughout the retirement literature is the inadequacy of data bases. Most of the large, influential studies of retirement, for men and women, use data from the Retirement History Survey (RHS) (Slevin & Wingrove, 1995; Weaver, 1994; Leonesio, 1993; Hayward & Grady, 1990; McBride, 1988; Gratton & Haug, 1983). This longitudinal survey was prepared by the Social Security Administration over the period of 1969 to 1979. It documents the retirement behavior of respondents who were born during 1905–1911. Several methodological problems are inherent in the use of the RHS database especially as it relates to the study of women's retirement: (1) the data base offers little information about women reaching retirement age; (2) it contains no information on health status or pension (other than Social Security) income for women; (3) it is based on a cohort of men and women who were socialized during a previous era when traditional gender roles explained some of their retirement decisions; (4) the study only sampled unmarried women—married women were not independently surveyed due to their weaker attachment to the labor force in 1970; and (5) the study did not collect data on the presence of elderly parents or dependent children or spouse (Talaga & Beehr, 1995; Weaver, 1994; McBride, 1988; Gratton and Haug, 1983). The majority of studies on women's retirement have used the RHS database making findings highly circumspect for use with future cohort groups such as baby boom women. Hope for the future study of women's retirement can be found in the new databases, the Health and Retirement Study (HRS) and the National Longitudinal Survey of Mature Women (NLSMW). Both are just now generating high quality data; these two databases should solve some of the serious data problems associated with the study of women's retirement (Gustman et al., 1995; Gustman & Steinmeier, 1994; Weaver, 1994; Hayward & Grady, 1990).

The impending retirement of the baby boom generation will compel researchers to redefine the meaning of retirement. The diversity of the baby boom necessitates new research models utilizing methods that recognize generational assumptions, labor force experience and gender differences. Hayward and Grady (1990) urge researchers to consider a "cohort-based approach" to study retirement for both men and women. Comparisons of cohort biographies would make it possible to examine shifts in underlying labor force behavior and factor in generational characteristics. There is also a need to make visible gender and class relations. Calasanti (1993) recommends a socialist-feminist approach in order to expose where and under what circumstances the causes and consequences of retirement produce variances by gender, race/ethnicity and class. How gender relations shape retirement experiences will provide insight into the similarities and differences between baby boom men and women.

The literature is far behind women's work experience and the social changes brought on by the massive entry of women into the labor force (Calasanti, 1993; Fox, 1984). Inherent in most studies of women's retirement has been the premise that a man's status and identity is obtained through work while a woman's social position is derived primarily through her family roles (Erdner and Guy, 1990). Women have been treated as adjuncts to men, never as the center of analysis (Slevin & Wingrove, 1995; Calasanti, 1992; Hess, 1990). The structures that propelled this belief are evidenced by how and what data have been collected about women's retirement. Very little is known about the retirement behavior of women (Slevin & Wingrove, 1995; Talaga & Beehr, 1995; Szinovacz & Washo, 1992; McBride, 1988). Information regarding married women's actual retirement plans and circumstances is virtually non-existent (Wise, 1990); reflecting the long-standing assumption that married women's retirement was irrelevant. This assumption of retirement's unimportance to women's lives, especially married women, continued until the 1980s (Slevin & Wingrove, 1995; Wise, 1990; Gratton & Haug, 1983; Szinovacz, 1982). Ironically, married baby boom women have been the vanguard of labor market changes in the post-industrial economy. The changing status of women's roles over the past two decades now makes retirement important for working women; it has also outdated and made obsolete existing retirement data (Slevin & Wingrove, 1995; Weaver, 1994; Erdner and Guy, 1990). To accurately reflect retirement's relevancy and importance in their lives, future study will need to be vigilant in the reformulation of the definition and meaning of retirement for women. Research models that expose the unique aspects of women's work and life histories are needed to effectively predict their future retirement experience.

Women's Retirement

A noticeable increase in the volume of research on women's retirement began in the late 1970s (Slevin & Wingrove, 1995; Szinovacz, 1982). This was most likely triggered by the impressive labor force participation rates of baby boom women. Recent literature reviews on the work and retirement decisions of older women reveal the growing recognition of the importance of women to the labor market. Although severely handicapped by the quality of research, existing studies in the literature can help formulate general hypotheses about the future retirement of baby boom women.

The literature on women's retirement focuses on the impact of family environment (e.g., retirement decisions of husband, spouse's health, dependent children/parents, etc.) and financial status (asset, pension and Social Security wealth—own and husband's—work experience/wage rate, etc.). Family is taken as the referent for women's work and retirement (Calasanti, 1993). The key predictors of retirement for women, both married and single, hinge on relationships to other individuals, specifically family and spouse (Talaga & Beehr, 1995; Gustman & Steinmeier, 1994; Weaver, 1994; Pozzebon & Mitchell, 1989; McBride, 1988). Talaga and Beehr (1995) attribute the heavy influence of others in the retirement decision to the traditional social role of women as nurturers and emotional providers for others. Calasanti (1993) contends that the retirement models are substantively different for men and women. When women are studied a "gender" model is used, which treats paid work in relation to family; when men are studied a "job" model is used, which treats paid work as central to men's lives, influencing all other dimensions, including family relationships. Women's role as society's caregivers presumes that the private realm is factored into the prediction equation.

The key predictors investigated by researchers can be organized into four basic categories: Family and Spouse Effects; Financial Effects; Work Effects; Health Effects (see Table 3). The study of family and spouse effects appears to dominate the literature, followed by financial effects. While not as frequently studied, there is acknowledgment that employment history and job characteristics strongly influence women's retirement decisions (Feuerbach & Erdwins, 1994; McBride, 1988).

To illustrate the perplexing status of the current literature, four studies are examined and contrasted: Campione's (1987) study, McBride's (1988) survey, Feuerbach and Erdwins's (1994) research on retirement attitudes and Slevin & Wingrove's (1995) analysis. All studies are concerned with identifying gender differences in the retirement process. Each study looked at (utilizing different methods) married women's retirement behavior. The authors' findings have been extracted and summarized in Table 4. Comparison of their results of selected family and spouse effects demonstrates the confusion and contradictions that exist in the study of older women's work and retirement decisions. All four studies used the three variables listed in Table 4—retirement status of husband, health status of husband, and presence of dependents in the household, children or parents—as predictors of women's retirement decisions. Each study concluded whether the variable was a predictor (yes) or was not a predictor (no) of a woman's decision to retire.

Table 3
Key Predictors Found in Women's Retirement Literature

Family and Spouse Effects	Financial Effects
Husband retired	Asset wealth
Husband in poor health	Own pension wealth
Presence of dependent children	Husband's pension wealth
Presence of dependent parents	Social Security wealth
Joint retirement decisions	Paid work
Work Effects	**Health Effects**
Employment history	Personal health status
Occupation	
Wage rate	

Campione's and Feuerbach and Erdwins's findings imply that family plays a limited role in the work and retirement decisions of women;

McBride concludes that family and spouse characteristics are important factors in the retirement process; Talaga and Beehr surmise that family and spouse variables are the most significant predictors of women's retirement. All studies reported that the retirement status of the husband influenced the retirement decision of married women. No consensus was reached on either of the other two variables. All authors advise extreme caution about the results of their findings and note the data and methodological problems. Campione's and McBride's studies most likely are affected by generational bias while both Feuerbach and Erdwins's and Talaga and Beehr's work was based on very small samples. Further, Feuerbach and Erdwins's study was an attitude survey of employed, married women nearing customary retirement age; their results reflect attitudes not actual behavior. All four studies raise as many questions as they attempt to answer.

Table 4
Comparison of Selected Criteria from Four Studies on Women's Retirement

	Campione (1987)	McBride (1988)	Feuerbach & Erdwins (1994)	Talaga & Beehr (1995)
Selected Family and Spouse Effects	Analysis of Data From the Panel Study	Survey of Cohort of Women Who First Received Retired-Worker Social Security Benefits, June, 1980 to May, 1981	Sample Study of 149 Married Career Women	Random Sample of Older Employees and Retirees from a Large Midwestern Manu-facturing Organization
• retirement status of husband	Yes	Yes	Yes	Yes
• health status of husband	No	No	No	No
• presence of dependents in the household, children or parents	No	Yes	No	Yes

Table 4 illustrates the problem of definition and operationalization endemic to the study of women's retirement. Disclaimers abound in the literature to warn the reader of these problems. The pervasiveness of this dilemma makes it extremely difficult for researchers to rely on reported findings.

Current studies of women's retirement may lack specificity, clarity and consistency but they do offer insights into the retirement future of baby boom women. Variables that bear consideration for future study of baby boom women's retirement are:

- Family needs will establish key criteria for both married and unmarried women. Conventional wisdom dictates that just as family has influenced female baby boom labor force participation, so it will influence their retirement experience (see Chapter 4). Demographic changes and the aging of the U.S. population will have bearing on baby boom women's retirement (see Chapter 3).

- Wives are less likely to retire while their husbands are working and vice-versa. Joint retirement of spouses, especially if the spouses are close in age, will be part of the prediction equation.

- Diminished or poor health will continue as a strong, influential variable.

- Women with greater work experience are less likely to retire early. Structural conditions of women's labor force participation will offer strong clues about future retirement behavior.

- Women who draw high wages are less likely to retire. Financial reward for work (wages) is an important determinant of labor force participation or retirement for both married and unmarried women.

CONCLUSION

The search for the "best way" to define and measure retirement is the single biggest challenge for the future study of retirement. The need for the reformulation of analytical categories including the very meaning of the concept of retirement is quite clear (Calasanti, 1993). Women's retirement literature is a relatively new field of study and as such is experiencing growing pains (Hatch & Thompson, 1992b). However, the evolution of women's retirement literature may serve as the catalyst to alter how retirement, for both men and women, is studied in the United States.

As with the general literature on retirement, most of the studies on women's retirement are atheoretical. It also places heavy emphasis on social-psychological analyses versus structural analyses (Slevin & Wingrove, 1995). Feminist authors contend that an examination of structural processes would reflect the inequities women experience in the labor market. Structural analysis would allow researchers to search for similarities and differences (both subtle and obvious) between men and women. Inherent in feminist analyses is the assumption that women have dissimilar work and retirement experiences from men. Even if women have comparable levels of education or income, their social and family role commitments will make their retirement experience different. Calasanti (1993) contends that a dialectic approach to how retirement is viewed is needed; the context of work/family relations is imperative to understand women's, as well as, men's retirement. Hatch and Thompson (1992b) suggest that women's retirement would be more effectively studied if: (1) multiple measures of retirement, subjective and objective, were utilized; and (2) retirement is conceptualized in terms of gradation or degrees.

In 1983, Gratton and Haug wrote "we have little idea why women retire." To further the study of women's retirement, they advised:

- the research be based on large samples that provide extensive data on sample members and their spouses;

- a longitudinal design;

- careful collection of health and attitudinal data.

More than a decade later, the above quote still applies to the state of women's retirement research. Little progress has been made to solve the data and methodological problems confronting the study of women's retirement even though expectations are high for the new databases, the Health and Retirement Study (HRS) and the National Longitudinal Survey of Mature Women (NLSMW). Future research will need to account for the dual roles (wage earner and homemaker/caretaker) of baby boom women. The field has become more complex, resulting in a strong demand for theoretical and methodological approaches that account for macro and micro level influences in the retirement decision.

The intent of this book is to further the study of women's retirement. Prospects for the study of baby boom women's retirement are exciting but limited. While a reliable blueprint for retirement may not be possible, insight into new dimensions of study may better understanding of what retirement will be for baby boom women.

3

Our Aging Population and
Its Effect on Women's Retirement

Changes in the population age structure will frame and mold the retirement experience for baby boom women. The focus of this chapter is to assess how population aging will impact the retirement of baby boom women. Understanding how this demographic trend will trigger social changes on the macro and micro level is important to accurately forecast what retirement will be for baby boom women.

There is a general consensus among demographers, and within the current literature, that the population of the United States is aging, along a path similar to that of other advanced industrial countries. The population aging literature concerns itself, primarily, with the following issues: the impact population aging will have on future population growth and, in turn, on economic growth; projections about the future size and makeup of the labor force; forecasts about the cost of population aging, specifically, the increased financial pressure population aging will place on social insurance programs; and the implications on social policy (i.e., how to support a growing older population and how to ensure a fair and equitable distribution of resources). According to the objectives of this chapter, population data will be viewed through a different lens, shifting specifically to baby boom women.

Changes in a population's median age reflect the process of population aging. As seen in Table 5, in 1950, the median age in the United States was 30.2 years with a relatively young population of 152 million. In 1990, the median age was 32.8 years of age with a total population of 250 million. Based on the middle series projections prepared by the Bureau of the Census, the population in 2030 will be double that of the 1950 population. The median age, from 1990 to 2030, will increase nine years to 41.8 years (Aging America, 1991). Although population projections are often viewed with some skepticism, demographers today agree that the U.S. population will continue to age. The reason this can be said with certainty is that the majority of the population that is expected to be around in the next 20–30 years is already here (Rappaport & Schieber, 1993). The median age of the U.S. population will continue to rise—the question is how slowly or how quickly. The answer to that question is contingent upon the assumptions one makes about population growth.

Table 5
Median Age of the United States Population

Date	Median Age	Population
1950	30.2	152 million
1990	32.8	250 million
2030	41.8	301 million (middle series)

Source: *1994 Statistical Abstract of the United States; Aging America: Trends and Projections*, United States Department of Commerce. 1994.

Population aging has social and economic significance because of its impact upon individual behavior affecting economic and other characteristics of a population and its economy (e.g., relative number of persons of dependent or working age, capacity for work, productivity, income distribution, consumption patterns, etc.) (Clark, et al., 1978). Characteristics of an aging population include: a significant rise in the 65 and over population; a sharp rise in median age; a larger fraction of the "old-old" or those over the age of 85; falling birth rates; and a decline in the proportion of children in the population. To determine the age structure of a population three variables are analyzed—fertility, immigration and mortality. As a cohort group, baby boom women have had and will continue to have significant influence on the aging of the United States population because of their contribution to two of the three variables—fertility and mortality.

FERTILITY

Since 1950, all advanced industrial countries have experienced significant population aging (Clark, 1993). Two distinct processes are causing population aging in developed countries: (1) declining fertility at or below replacement levels; and (2) increased life expectancy. The effects of both processes result in what demographers call the double aging process—the shrinking numbers of younger persons occurring simultaneously with the expanding numbers of the elderly (Borsch-Supan, 1992). The population of the United States will experience this double aging process well into the twenty-first century.

The most unpredictable component of population projection is fertility. The reason the fertility rate is so volatile is that it involves individual choice and that choice can be influenced by many social and economic factors as well as by social class, and ethnic and generation characteristics (Preston, 1993). It is for this reason that the decision a baby boom woman makes about childbearing will be one of the more important factors in determining her retirement life, both at the macro and micro level.

A turnaround in fertility can seriously distort current population projections. It is the uncertainty and volatility associated with fertility that allowed the baby boom to catch demographers by surprise (Light, 1988). As one demographer described it, "Simply put, the baby boom was a 'disturbance' which emanated from a decade-and-a-half-long fertility splurge on the part of American couples. This post-WWII phenomenon upset what had been a century-long decline in the U.S. fertility rate" (Bouvier & DeVita, 1980). The fertility decline resumed again at the end of the baby boom in the mid-1960s. For the United States, the behavior of fertility will determine the age composition of its population (Clark, 1978).

Demographers utilize the TFR—Total Fertility Ratio to measure and project fertility rates. The total fertility ratio is the number of births that 1000 women would have in their lifetime if, at each year of age, they experienced the birth rates occurring in the specified year. A total fertility rate of 2,110 represents "replacement level" fertility for the total population under current mortality conditions, assuming no net immigration (U.S. 1994 Statistical Abstract). Until the baby boom period, the Total Fertility Rate had steadily declined. In the 1930s, it hit then-historic lows, hovering just above the replacement level of 2.1 children per woman. The baby boom, of course, changed this pattern. Between 1947 and 1964, TFRs ranged between 3.1 and 3.7 (Bouvier & DeVita, 1991). However, the TFR began to drop abruptly during the mid-1960s and dipped below replacement level for the first time ever in U.S. history in 1972 and by 1976 hit an historic low of 1.7. The TFR remained fairly stable at approximately 1.8 during the 1980s, until 1987 when it began to edge upwards. In 1990, the TFR was estimated at 2.08—just below replacement level.

The recent rise in birth rates in the late 1980s and early 1990s (Table 6) has been attributed to the increase of women in their 30s who are now having children after a delay to establish work careers. In 1990, women aged 30 and older accounted for 30% of the total births (American Demographics, 1994). This is viewed as a temporary departure from the downward slope of fertility rates. It is not currently seen as an indication of increasing fertility.

Table 6
Total and Projected Fertility Rates, 1960–1990 (Per 1,000 Women)

Annual Average and Year	Total Fertility Rate	Annual Average and Year	Total Fertility Rate
1960–64	3.45	1980–84	1.81
1965–69	2.62	1985–88	1.87
1970–74	2.09	1989	2.01
1975–79	1.77	1990	2.08

Source: Adapted from *1994 Statistical Abstract*, United States Department of Commerce, 1994.

Future projections about the fertility rate have been argued along theoretical positions. The more popular media view is Easterlin's theory of birth and fortune—the size of a generation shapes the social and economic conditions of society and, subsequently, the life choices of individuals. The birth rate of the baby boomers has and will remain at below replacement level because its large cohort size has created unfavorable economic and social conditions—crowded labor market, housing market, etc. (Easterlin, 1987; Preston, 1993). According to Easterlin's theory, therefore, the baby bust generation will have a higher fertility rate than the baby boom generation because its small size will generate more advantageous economic and social opportunities.

Easterlin's theory is often criticized as "demographic determinism" by those who take the other dominant position on fertility projections, that is, that the fertility rate will resume its long-term downward trend (Bumpass, 1990). Easterlin's critics argue that effects of population structure on social behavior may not be as direct as demographic or economic determinism would suggest. They contend that social and economic conditions are relevant and should be linked to the strength of demographic relationships. Pampel (1993) does not reject Easterlin's theory but argues that social and institutional characteristics such as high rates of female labor force participation will contribute to the declining influence of relative cohort size on fertility.

Both the Social Security Administration and the Bureau of the Census project ultimate total fertility rates of 1.9 births and 1.8 births, respectively, per woman through the first half of the 21st century (Rappaport & Schieber, 1993). Structural changes in the economy and changes in social behavior almost preclude another significant baby boom or boomlet. The greater share of women in the labor force, later ages at marriage, continued high divorce rates, ability to control the number and spacing of births, etc., suggest that the fertility rate will not exceed replacement level. The life choices made by baby boom women have resulted in a fertility rate that will continue the aging of the population. This demographic characteristic demonstrates the tremendous power that fertility changes have on the age structure of American society (Riche, 1993).

While the majority of baby boom women are beyond their childbearing years, some, especially those who have delayed childbirth, are just beginning their childbearing years. An historic-high number of baby boom women who have children or who are currently in their childbearing years are working outside the home—three out of four baby boom women are in the labor force. In addition, a significant share of these women are not married. In absolute numbers, baby boom women will have a large number of babies—American women gave birth to more than 4 million babies in 1990, more than in any year since 1961. It is estimated that about 85% of baby boom women will bear children. According to the U.S. Bureau of Census in 1991, three out of four baby boom women have had children, ranging from 80% of the oldest boomers to about 60% of the youngest. However, baby boom women have not made the commitment to childbearing to the degree that their mothers did. Childlessness was rare among their mothers. For example, only 8% of women born in the 1930s were childless.

Although the cohort group will have many children, in terms of fertility rates, the baby boomers will, at best, replace themselves. Baby boom women have created a demographic paradox—a record number of women in the childbearing ages are still bearing record-small families. Riche (1993) argues that this paradox can be explained by a significant trend among baby boom women—more women are having and/or raising children on their own. The U.S. National Center for Health Statistics (1991) has reported that almost all recent increase in fertility has occurred among women who were not currently married.

The fertility behavior of baby boom women has obvious macro level implications for population aging, primarily the determination of replacement ratios. However, looking beyond appearances, baby boom women's fertility decisions clearly impact other social structures. First, baby boom women, unlike their mothers and grandmothers, have been and are making new and different decisions about childbearing. Baby boom women have chosen to have children later in life, to have fewer children and, for some, to bear children without being married first. Their behavior can be attributed to a changing social milieu, which has given baby boom women control over their fertility, their financial status, their education—while lifting taboos about divorce, bearing children out of wedlock, singlehood, etc. These new options to childbearing have led some demographers to suggest that birth rates, today and in the future, will be the result of decisions made by women rather than by couples. Regardless, a demographic universal appears to have formulated: baby boom women will have an average of close to two children, even knowing that they will be faced with work-family conflicts.

Second, as a cohort group, it appears that baby boom women have created what Karl Mannheim refers to as a new "Zeitgeist," or shared feeling, about the social role of women in childbirth and child rearing. A clear pattern appears to have emerged from this new "Zeitgeist," which will have significant impact on the future of retirement for baby boom women.   For the mothers and grandmothers of baby boom women, childbearing and marriage were synonymous. For baby boom women it is not. Baby boom women have opted to have children despite the high level of marital instability in the United States. The decision to bear children, knowing that they may be the sole supporter of their children, is an emerging demographic pattern that will shape the retirement of baby boom women.

For the mothers and grandmothers of baby boom women, marriage was the key structural variable to predict their retirement experience. Marriage was the best (and perhaps only) indicator of an adequate retirement for women since they were dependent on the retirement income gained from their husbands. The conspicuous lack of data, information or study of women's retirement supports the position that no attention was given to women's retirement since it was considered a subset of men's retirement. Social and fiscal policies that shaped the institution of retirement assumed that older women would be provided for because of the institution of marriage. That assumption worked well for the majority of the mothers of baby boomers since an enduring marriage was a social norm. Women born during the late 1920s and 1930s married at a higher rate than previous cohorts of women. For example, 96% of those born in the 1930s married, compared to 92% of those born between 1900 and 1909 (Russell, 1982).

Changes in pension coverage, economic restructuring, women's labor force participation and divorce rates for baby boomers have minimized marriage as a key structural variable for predicting baby boom women's retirement. Unlike their mothers, baby boom women will not be able to depend exclusively on the retirement income from their husbands (see Chapter 5). Marriage will continue to be a variable in predicting women's retirement but it will not hold the financial and social significance it did for their mothers. Marriage will be an advantage, not a guarantee of a secure retirement.

MORTALITY

The other significant component influencing population aging, in the context of discussing the future retirement of baby boom women, is mortality. Although demographers argue about the best technique to determine mortality projections, mortality is the least controversial of the assumptions since there are natural biological limits to the life span. The twentieth century has seen death rates drop steadily, resulting in increased life expectancy. The first half of the century saw the most dramatic reductions in deaths of infants and children due to medical advances against infectious diseases. The average life expectancy of a baby born in 1900 was 47.3 years; in 1990, a baby can be expected to live on average for 75.5 years (AARP, 1993a). The cause for increases in life expectancy in the second half of this century has been due to declines in mortality among the middle aged and the elderly. Women and the elderly aged 85+ years have seen the most dramatic reductions in mortality primarily due to successful treatment of cardiovascular diseases (Taeuber & Allen, 1993). Mortality improvements for persons aged 65 years and older are projected to continue into the 21st century (Preston, 1993).

Mortality declines, coupled with replacement level fertility rates, have increased the momentum of population aging. So much so that the age structure of the United States, like other advanced industrial countries, is shifting from a pyramid-like structure (relatively small group of older persons, a middling number of middle-aged people in the middle, and many young adults, teenagers, and children at the bottom) to a pillar-like structure (three roughly equal age groups—youth, middle-aged, and the

mature).   As recently as 1970, the pyramid model was a good
representation of our population but because of the baby boom
phenomenon itself, the decrease in fertility rates since 1965, and extended
life expectancy, the pillar model will be the long-term image of the age
structure of the population.

As Figures 2–4 illustrate, the older population (65+) has been slowly
growing since 1960. It will continue to grow at a steady pace until the
year 2020 when it will experience considerable growth due to the leading
edge of the baby boomers entering the older population. Growth will
become most pronounced when all baby boomers have reached the age of
65, by 2030, and will comprise about 21% of the total U.S. population
(Table 7). That year, the youngest baby boomers will have passed their
65th birthday and the oldest boomers will be on the verge of their 85th.
By 2040, the largest segment of the older population will be baby boom
women aged 85+.

Figure 2
U.S. Population, by Age and Sex, 1960

Source: Bouvier & DeVita. "The Baby Boom—Entering Midlife." *Population Bulletin*.
26, no. 3 (November, 1991).

Figure 3
U.S. Population, by Age and Sex, 1990

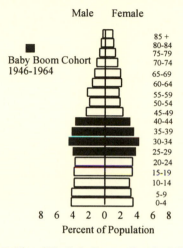

Source: Bouvier & DeVita. "The Baby Boom—Entering Midlife." *Population Bulletin.*
26, no. 3 (November, 1991).

Figure 4
U.S. Population, by Age and Sex, 2040

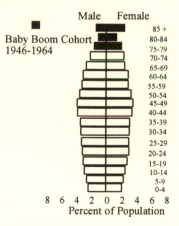

Source: Bouvier & DeVita. "The Baby Boom—Entering Midlife." *Population Bulletin.*
26, no.3 (November, 1991).

Table 7
Actual and Projected Growth of the Older Population, 1990–2050 (Numbers in Millions)

Yr.	Total popul. all ages	55 to 64 yrs		65 to 74 yrs		75 to 84 yrs		85+ yrs		65+ yrs	
		#	%	#	%	#	%	#	%	#	%
1990	248 m	20.1	8.5	18.0	7.3	10.0	4.0	3.0	1.2	31.1	12.5
2000	276 m	23.7	8.6	18.6	6.7	12.4	4.5	4.3	1.6	35.3	12.8
2010	300 m	34.6	11.5	21.0	7.0	13.2	4.4	6.0	2.0	40.1	13.3
2020	325 m	42.3	13.0	30.9	9.5	15.5	4.7	7.0	2.1	53.3	16.3
2030	349 m	37.4	10.7	38.0	10.9	23.3	6.7	8.8	2.5	70.2	**20.0**
2040	371 m	37.7	10.1	34.0	9.1	29.2	7.9	13.8	3.7	77.0	20.7
2050	392 m	42.9	10.9	34.6	8.8	26.6	6.8	19.0	4.8	80.1	20.4

Note: Excludes armed forces overseas. Projections are taken from the middle series.
Source: Adapted from *1994 Statistical Abstract*, United States Department of Commerce, 1994.

Most baby boomers can expect to live nearly two full decades past their retirement from paid work, assuming the current retirement age of 65. Baby boomers will make it to their retirement, in the first place, in large part because they survived their very first year of life (Light, 1988). Baby boomers have made significant changes in their health habits by not smoking, using seatbelts, and exercising. Demographers do not yet know what the impact on life expectancy will be if they pursue their healthful habits into old age. On the other hand, baby boom women entering the labor force in record numbers has resulted in their adopting risk-taking behaviors similar to men, evidenced by the recent narrowing of the difference between men's and women's life expectancy (Riche, 1993). Table 8 highlights the differences in life expectancy between baby boom men and women at age 65. Even though the gender gap in life expectancy will contract as the baby boom moves into old age, women will still be more likely than men to survive to the oldest ages. Baby boom women can therefore plan on a longer period of retirement than their male counterparts.

Gerontologists categorize the elderly into three age categories—the young-old, which is the age group from 65–74; the middle-old, the age group from 75–84; and the old-old, 85 years and older. The most significant demographic change we will see with population aging is the stunning growth of the old-old (85+) age group, most of whom are women. The number of old-old increased fivefold from 1950 to 1990.

In 1990, the old-old numbered about 3 million; in 2030, assuming Census Bureau middle series projections, the number will be 8.8 million and by 2040, there will be nearly 13.8 million old-old baby boomers (Table 7). Almost two-thirds of that age group (63.0%) will be women (Table 9).

Table 8
Projected Life Expectancy at Birth and Age 65, by Sex, 1990–2040 (in Years)

Year	At Birth			At Age 65		
	Men	Women	Differ- ence	Men	Women	Differ- ence
1990	72.1	79.0	6.9	15.0	19.4	4.4
2000	73.5	80.4	6.9	15.7	20.3	4.6
2010	74.4	81.3	6.9	16.2	21.0	4.8
2020	74.9	81.8	6.9	16.6	21.4	4.8
2030	75.4	82.3	6.9	17.0	21.8	4.8
2040	75.9	82.8	6.9	17.3	22.3	5.0

Source: Adapted from U.S. Bureau of the Census. "Projections of the Population of the United States, by Age, Sex, and Race: 1988 to 2080," by Gregory Spencer. *Current Population Reports* Series P-25, No. 1018 (January, 1989).

Demographers are very concerned about the impact mortality declines are having on population aging. In fact, the two most discussed statistics associated with population aging are the old-age dependency ratio (the number of elderly persons per 100 people aged 18–64) and the overall dependency ratio (the number of elderly persons plus children under age 18 per 100 people aged 18–64). Although attention is often confined to old-age dependency, changes in dependency must be put into proper perspective. Cowgill notes that most advanced industrial countries, all with relatively aged populations, have quite low dependency loads, much lower than developing nations (Riche, 1993). Recent projections from the United Nations support this finding. The double aging process in the United States will generate overall dependency ratios for the first half of the 21st century which, barring radical changes in immigration policy or mortality conditions, "are not out of line with what has been experienced in the past century" (Easterlin, 1991). The United States has already lived through an upsurge in dependency in the 1960s when the baby boom was in infancy and childhood. It will experience another dependency peak in 2040 when the entire cohort group is retired.

Easterlin (1991) and Schulz (1992) challenge much of the negative analysis that has been done about future dependency ratios. They argue that the doomsayers use simplistic dependency ratios without incorpor-ating economic analysis into their projections. Schulz labels this "a kind of voodoo demographics." Both authors conclude that the future overall support burden will be less in the years 2030–2050, baby boom retirement years, than it was during 1950–1970, the baby boom's childhood. As Figure 5 illustrates, the total dependency ratio will not exceed the level it attained in 1964 at the height of the baby boom even with all baby boomers having reached age 65 in 2030.

Table 9
Projected Population of Older (65+) Baby Boom Population by Sex, Year 2040 (in Thousands)

Year	Age	Men		Women		% Totals	Total	
		#	%	#	%		#	%
	65 to 74	16,174	47.6	17,794	52.4	100.0	33,968	44.1
2040	75 to 84	13,566	46.4	15,640	53.6	100.0	29,206	37.9
	85+	5,116	37.0	8,724	**63.0**	100.0	13,840	18.0
								100.0

Note: Excludes armed forces overseas. Projections are taken from the middle series.
Source: Adapted from *1994 Statistical Abstract*, United States Department of Commerce, 1994.

The more pertinent question regarding future dependency ratios is how will changes in dependency composition (youth dependency is declining as old-age dependency is increasing) impact the total economic burden of dependency on the working age population? Current research on the relative dependency costs of the young and the old reports that total expenditure per dependent is not much different for older than for younger dependents (Easterlin, 1991). What will occur are shifts in fund allocation (e.g., from education to health care). If these findings hold true, predictions about the economic, political and intergenerational struggles resulting from the projected economic burden imposed by the retirement of the baby boom may not materialize. Both authors contend that more research based on recent data is needed to make better projections about the impact of future dependency ratios.

Using the filter of baby boom women's retirement, discussion about mortality declines shifts away from the macro, dependency issue, to a micro perspective. Mortality declines and changes in dependency composition will produce two fundamental facts that will impact baby boom women's retirement—one demographic and the other the continuation of current social policy: (1) baby boom women, like their mothers, can expect to be alone in their old age; and (2) they will be required by society to be the primary care providers of the country's frail elderly before and throughout their retirement years before becoming frail themselves.

If a baby boom woman reaches age 65, she can expect to live until age 85 (Table 8). For the majority of that time, she will be alone as a widow, a divorcé or as never married. She will likely be widowed at the age of 67 and remain a widow for fifteen years. Fewer than one in ten will remarry (U.S. Department of Commerce, 1991). According to Social Security Administration projections, by 2040, there will be 15 million widows and 4.5 million widowers aged 65 or older. Although baby boom women and their mothers will share the experience of single living in their old age, it is questionable whether their living arrangements will follow the same pattern.

Figure 5
Dependency Ratios of Children and Elderly, 1950–2030

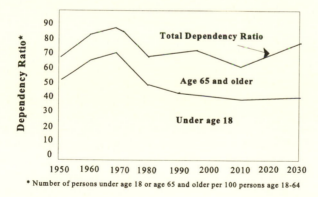

* Number of persons under age 18 or age 65 and older per 100 persons age 18-64

Source: Bouvier & DeVita. "The Baby Boom–Entering Midlife." *Population Bulletin.* 26, no. 3 (November, 1991).

In 1992, the majority (67%) of older persons lived in a family setting. For men and women age 65+, 81% and 56%, respectively, lived with their spouses or other family members (AARP, 1993a). Forty-two percent of older women lived alone, and as they age this percentage will increase. Studies indicate that elderly Americans prefer to live apart from their children and remain independent for as long as possible. In 1986, only 14% of the aged were living with one or more of their children or with another non-spouse relative (U.S. Senate Special Committee on Aging, 1991). The decision to move in with relatives remains an act of financial or social necessity rather than preference (Schulz, 1992). It is unclear whether the current trend of elderly women living alone will continue for baby boom women. Financial status and health status determines whether an older person will live alone. More than three-quarters of households headed by older persons owned their own home in 1992. Older male householders were more likely to be owners (85%) than were females (68%). In 1990, only 55% of all baby boomers owned their own home. Home ownership does increase with age; that is, two-thirds of the older baby boom owned a home in 1990, while fewer than half (44%) of younger boomers did. However, only 36% of baby boom women owned homes compared to 63% of baby boom men (Bouvier & DeVita, 1991). This may be a telling statistic about the future living arrangements for baby boom women. Today's elderly women have the financial option to choose to live alone since a significant number of them own homes. Married baby boom women who are home owners are more likely to have the option of living alone than divorced or never-married women or non-home owners.

Population aging will concentrate older persons at the more extreme elderly ages, where chronic health conditions become more prevalent and activity limitations increase the need for long-term care. Improved survival rates imply a shift from acute disease to chronic illnesses. Half of all persons age 85 or older (who are not institutionalized) require assistance with activities of daily living—eating, bathing, dressing, walking, etc. Chronic illnesses increase with age and are more common among women. Functional limitations, brought on by chronic illnesses such as arthritis, hypertension, heart conditions, osteoporosis, etc., are higher for women than men and increase with age (Taeuber & Allen, 1993). The onset of chronic illnesses and the shorter life expectancy of men will ensure that baby boom women will have more years of expected dependency than men. Since the majority of elderly baby boom women will not have a spouse for assistance, especially when their health declines, they will rely on their children and relatives for support and assistance in old age.

Although much of the discussion about population aging hinges on transfer programs like Social Security and Medicare, some gerontologists, like Robert Butler, former director of the National Institute on Aging, urge investment in research designed to reduce frailty and delay the onset of chronic illnesses, which will increase independence later in life (Kingson, 1991). If medical advances appear that will delay or minimize the effects of chronic illness for baby boom women, their reliance on their children (due to health status) may be postponed to some degree.

The second fundamental fact baby boom women will deal with as an effect of population aging and mortality declines is the implicit social contract that they will be the primary care providers for the elderly. Studies that report that the American "family" is the number one caretaker of the elderly in this country are somewhat misleading. What they really mean is that American "women" are the care providers for the nation's elderly because they are the ones who actually deliver the hands-on care. This social fact will remain steady especially if social transfer programs and programs for the elderly continue to be diluted through legislative and budgetary actions. The main mechanisms relied upon in the United States to transfer resources from working to nonworking persons are the family, the private sector (employers), and the government. The assumption implied, when justifying scaling back state and federally sponsored programs for the elderly, is that additional burdens will shift to the family but, in reality, it will shift to women.

The dramatic increase in the old-old population makes it likely that older people will themselves have at least one surviving parent, uncle, aunt, brother or sister, etc., who will need some type of support or assistance. The overwhelming majority of the nation's elderly live in their communities. Only a small number (5%) of today's elderly population are institutionalized or live in nursing homes (U.S. Senate Special Committee on Aging, 1991). This trend will continue as society encourages and promotes elderly independence and family care because of the cost of hospitalization, nursing homes and home care services.

Families are the support providers for frail and disabled older people, both financially and with the activities of daily living. For older married couples, the spouse usually serves as the primary caregiver. When the older person is widowed or not married, an adult daughter or daughter-in-law is generally the caregiver. Generally speaking, women are more likely to provide care to their frail elderly parents in terms of time; men are more likely to provide financial help. In 1990, 44% of adult daughters (or daughters-in-law) who cared for an impaired parent were employed

(Bouvier & DeVita, 1991). If this pattern continues for the baby boom cohort, the young-old will be taking care of the old-old. This is especially likely since the parents of the baby boom began having children as young adults, in their early twenties. Work-family conflicts, similar to the childcare dilemmas they felt as young women, will again rear their heads as baby boom women become the young-old. Under the mantle of social and family obligations, baby boom women will feel the burden of old age dependency as they did with the strains of childcare and work. Many baby boom women may have to leave the work force or work part-time just when they will need to work for retirement benefits for their own old age or while they are adjusting to their own retirement, widowhood, and reduced incomes.

There is no historical precedent for the experience of most middle-aged and young-old people having living parents. In 1940, one in three 50-year-old women had living mothers, by 1980, that proportion had doubled to two in three. An indicator of the degree to which baby boom women will be asked to provide care for an older person is the parent support ratio (the number of persons aged 85+ per 100 persons aged 50 to 64 years). The parent support ratio tripled from 1950 to 1990 (from 3 to 9) and will triple again over the next six decades to 28 in 2050 (Taeuber & Allen, 1993). It is likely that a baby boom woman will acquire the role of care provider sometime during her pre-retirement and retirement years and then she herself will need care.

This demographic forecast is a double-edge sword for baby boom women. While they may look forward to living to a ripe old age, their retirement years will not be the life of leisure, travel, hobbies, etc., that perhaps their mothers enjoy today. "Paradox" seems to be the best word to describe baby boom women—they have created a demographic paradox with their childbearing choices, but they will be challenged with another demographic paradox—care for the nation's frail elderly and the old-old at a time when they themselves will be at a vulnerable point in their life. Baby boom women will not be prepared, at least financially, for the social role expected of them regarding the primary care of the country's elderly (see Chapter 5).

Current debate about population aging focuses on the economic burden of dependency on the working-age population. Both dominant theoretical positions—the gradual adjustment perspective or the intergenerational crisis perspective—formulate the issues within a financial context. Social policy is and will be framed by this dialectic and current interpretation of statistical forecasts and projections do not consider the social and financial consequences baby boom women will face. It is misleading not to recognize the compelling social role baby boom women will play during their retirement years in helping the country adjust to becoming an aging society. The debate must be expanded to include, explicitly, the macro and micro implications of population aging on all of society but particularly on baby boom women. Individual women need to be informed of the challenge they will be confronted with in an aging America.

SUMMARY

Population aging will inexorably alter baby boom women's expectations for retirement. If one looks beyond the observable facts or "appearances" that population aging currently suggests, several conclusions can be made about the future of retirement for baby boom women. Their fertility behavior has helped transform the institutions of marriage, family, and motherhood. It is therefore likely that it will also help shape their retirement years, especially as their life expectancy continues to increase. Baby boom women will continue their role as care providers with the shift from children to older persons. This dimension to their lives will heavily influence their labor force participation in their later middle years and into old age.

4

The Nature of Work and Its Impact on Baby Boom Women's Retirement

Any study of retirement must include a discussion of the nature of work since it factors into the retirement equation. This chapter will focus attention on how the nature of work determines the parameters for retirement, and specifically, the variables that will help determine the retirement scenarios of baby boom women. Retirement is considered an "earned" right, one attained by engaging in paid labor during early and middle adult life. The structure of labor markets, human capital investment, and social roles influence female labor force participation, all of which ultimately determine women's retirement experience.

This chapter begins with an historical overview of the development of work to provide context about baby boom women's labor force participation. Highlighting pertinent economic, social and historical trends will illustrate how past and present labor market conditions impact current work circumstances and retirement possibilities for baby boom women. It will shed light on what kinds of work they do, where they work, and, to some degree, why they work.

An in-depth look at the characteristics of baby boom women's labor force participation will follow. A step-by-step examination by age, race, education, marital status, presence of children, work status (full-time/part-time; hours of work), and occupation will be made. To identify similarities and differences, these variables will be compared with those affecting baby boom men and, when possible, other female cohort groups. The intent of this analysis is to examine the empirical data about baby boom women's labor force participation, going beyond casual observation to reveal a more accurate picture of work life for baby boom women.

The nature of work for baby boom women and their demographic characteristics will determine their future retirement decisions. This information will also help to identify and validate the macro level variables that will redefine the institution of retirement for the baby boom generation.

OVERVIEW: HISTORICAL DEVELOPMENT OF "WORK"

Work has had meaning, value and status since the beginning of civilization. The concept of work as "toil," and thus to be avoided, emerged from the formation of class structures. The landholding aristocracy believed any form of work ignoble. A contrasting view developed during the Middle Ages when the Church began teaching that both manual and intellectual labor were religious duties. The concept that work was ennobling began to shift from the monasteries to artisans and merchants. As the feudal system began to disintegrate, a class society developed: the nobility and wealthy, the upper class; the artisans, craftsmen, and merchants, the middle class; and the lower class, composed of serfs, menial laborers and servants. The concept of work became the foundation of society and formed the basis for social classes.

The Protestant Reformation promoted the value of work as a virtue. The social conditions created from this religious doctrine and from the development of a class structure supported the concept of work necessary to facilitate the Industrial Revolution. Environmental conditions in early America further solidified the notion that work was a moral obligation and the way to achieve one's salvation. Individuals who were non-productive or non-socially responsible were considered liabilities to be shunned and ostracized. Colonial agrarian society supported this notion of work. The elderly, while perhaps not directly involved in productive work, maintained their status in society and continued to be venerated primarily because they tended to be the property owners and the holders of wealth. Women's contribution to work during colonial times was considered very significant since the family was the primary economic unit. The new economy relied on "cottage industries" for production and the women who manufactured nearly all the articles used in daily life (Fox & Hesse-Biber, 1984).

The greatest changes in the nature of work began with the Civil War with the shift from an agrarian to an industrialized economy. The need for mass production generated by the war, coupled with technological advances, accelerated the spread of industrialism in the United States. The factory system overtook the cottage industry and fragmented work into specialized components. Machines replaced skilled labor with semi-skilled and unskilled labor. Frederick Taylor's theory of scientific management endorsed the notion that workers could be likened to machines. Efficiency was the goal; workers became machine tenders rather than artisans or creators. Speed and physical stamina replaced skill and experience as the criteria for the "ideal" worker. Industrialization brought workers greater fragmentation and specialization but also higher wages, a decrease in manual labor, a reduction in hours worked and an increase in leisure time.

Production moved from the home to the factory, effectively separating the home from the work place. This separation impacted the social status of both the elderly and women by excluding them from the paid labor force. Factory work required speed and stamina, qualities not attributed to the elderly or women. The net effect was to remove the elderly and women from the means of production, changing their social roles. The elderly were "retired" and women were designated to a support role. The ideology that a woman's place was in the home was taking a firm hold within society. However, during the early days of industrialization, demand for labor was strong and a steady supply of female workers was needed. The answer to this paradox was single women—whose employment was considered an interlude, a temporary step before marriage and motherhood (Fox & Hesse-Biber, 1984). Women continued to be part of the paid labor force, albeit on a conditional basis, while the elderly were removed from the work force via the emerging institution of retirement.

The process of industrialization facilitated the development of monopoly capitalism, a new system of control, altering the social relations of production. Industrialization was characterized by large-scale bureaucracies, an elaborate division of labor, and an emerging dual labor market. Monopoly capitalism produced primary and secondary labor markets: giant oligopolistic corporations in core industries with internal labor market mechanisms of stability and tenure, shadowed by subordinate, more competitive small businesses in peripheral industries relying on a surplus labor supply of contingent, low skilled or unskilled workers. These structural changes to the labor process and the labor market radically changed the nature of work. The compelling consequences for women and the elderly were found in the introduction of two parallel (seemingly contradictory) structural requirements: (1) the institution of retirement; and (2) a need for a reserve army of secondary market workers. Both experienced the de-valuation of their social status in American society. Women and the elderly shared similar fates—the elderly were dismissed from the paid labor force; women, while not completely dismissed, became almost invisible.

Retirement was created because organizations needed a mechanism to control entry and departure into the working world. Companies wanted to attract "ideal" candidates (primarily the young with speed and physical stamina) but needed to guarantee promotion and advancement to sustain their internal labor markets. Retirement quickly became society's formal mechanism to endorse, regulate and sanction the removal of the elderly from the paid labor force. It was further encouraged by the availability of Social Security retirement income. Retirement found a very receptive cord among American workers and was quickly adopted and integrated into the social structure of the United States. Industrialization witnessed the erosion of the American work ethic—intrinsic values of hard work and individual achievement—as workers were further removed from the production process. These changes in the nature of work made retirement attractive to the American worker, who felt he had earned the right to retire, even though retiring meant a decrease in social status.

While the elderly were leaving, women were joining the workplace. In spite of the ideal image perpetuated throughout American culture of women "at home" rather than "at work," women experienced a steady increase in labor force participation during the industrial era of the United States. The forces of industrialization created a need for a reserve army of workers to fill part-time, seasonal and marginal jobs. Women responded to this need and entered the paid labor force, albeit in low-status jobs.

Structural theory argues that dualistic industrial and labor market structures interacted with preexisting sex biases to relegate women to lower status occupations (Edwards, et al., 1975). Women entered primarily service occupations in the secondary labor market in clerical jobs, health and educational occupations or employment in peripheral manufacturing industries and retail trade. Although women steadily increased their labor force participation, for the overwhelming majority of working women, their employment in the secondary labor market ensured that their retirement experience would remain dependent on their spouse's retirement.

The shift from an industrial to a service/information economy is once again profoundly changing the nature of work. "Deindustrialization," "restructuring," "reengineering," "information age," "post-market era" are some of the terms being used to describe the new economic reality developing in the post-industrial era. Technology advances and workplace restructuring have facilitated productivity gains while downsizing and eliminating high-paid blue collar and middle-management jobs. Between 1979–1992, productivity increased by 35% in the manufacturing sector while its workforce shrank by 15% (Rifkin, 1995). American workers are facing new labor market conditions—a shift away from physically taxing jobs towards jobs that place priority on reasoning, analytical and language skills (Bluestone, et al., 1990). The labor market's occupational structure is being substantially reordered by the loss of high-wage, blue-collar jobs. This loss is not being offset by the creation of equally high paying work in the service sector. In fact, job creation has occurred predominately in the low-paying service sectors where much of the employment is temporary or part-time. The dual labor market structure has continued the gendered nature of employment. It is primarily women who are filling these low-paying jobs (Appelbaum & Schettkat, 1990).

In addition to the occupational structural changes, the nature of work has new meaning in a post industrial society. The new workplace has shattered the dream of company loyalty, long-term employment, job security, ladder-climbing careers, and comfortable retirement pensions. Well-paying jobs in the service, information and knowledge sectors require workers who are more highly skilled, educated and flexible. The workplace now demands that workers manage their own work life; careers will model webs, not ladders, requiring retraining, ongoing education and skill acquisition, and individual retirement planning and management. Financial self-reliance will be the challenge for the baby boom generation. Baby boom women need to manage the impact post industrial workplace transitions will have on their work life. These macro level changes in the workplace will influence the individual work life choices/decisions baby boom women make which, ultimately, will determine their retirement experience.

The nature of work is also being redefined by the demographic change that has accompanied this economic transformation to a post industrial society. The composition of the labor force has significantly changed, shifting from a white male majority to a majority of women and minorities. In 1940, women made up 24% of the total labor force; nearly three in ten women aged 16 years old and over were in the paid labor force. In 1994, women made up 46% of the total labor force; six of every ten women in the population aged 16 years old and over were in the paid labor force (Bureau of Labor Statistics, Report 892, July, 1995). Since their entry into the labor force, baby boom women have influenced the composition of the labor force more than any other cohort group. It is for this reason that their retirement behavior will become increasingly important. Many issues such as the future size of the labor force, the number of retirees, and the aggregate cost of Social Security benefits will hinge on the labor force participation and retirement behavior of baby boom women.

THE LABOR MARKET AND BABY BOOM WOMEN

Prior to the baby boom's entrance into the work force, women generally worked because they were single or poor. This pattern changed as baby boom women reached working age. Their attachment to the labor force dramatically increased due to many economic and social factors (i.e., higher educational attainment, a growing white-collar and service sector, changing social mores, rising divorce rates, delayed marriage, and lower fertility rates). By 1980, all baby boom women were in their early years of labor force participation and their entrance into the labor market vastly broadened the female attachment to the labor force beyond the single and poor woman. The most significant change in female labor force participation came from white women, more specifically, white, married women. Between 1975 and 1990, 15 million out of a total 31 million added to the labor force were white women (Fullerton, 1991). Baby boom women continued to be the vanguard for change through the decade of the '80s as they generated a striking increase in labor force participation among women with children (U.S. Department of Labor, 1994). Baby boom women created the "dual earner married couple." In 1994, only 17% of married couples had a 'traditional' arrangement with the husband in the labor force and the wife at home; in 1975, the figure was 42%.

Labor Force Participation

Work outside the home is the norm for baby boom women. A baby boom woman can expect to spend at least thirty years of her adult life in the paid labor force (Table 10). The peak years of labor force participation for baby boom women are between 1990–2005. Workers between the ages of 35–54 are considered to be at the peak of their productivity. Baby boom women will pass through their peak productivity years during this time.

The year 1990 will be the benchmark year used in this analysis to study baby boom women's labor force participation. The reasons for this are threefold: (1) women, in general, experienced their highest labor force participation rate (57.5%) of all time, in 1990 (U.S. Department of Labor,

1994); (2) the entire baby boom generation was in the 25–54 age group—allowing for the most accurate analysis of existing data collected and reported by the Bureau of Labor Statistics (see Chapter 3); and (3) baby boom women represented 54.1% of the female civilian labor force during 1990.

Table 10
Work Life Expectancy for Men and Women

	Men	Women
1960	41.1 yrs	20.1 yrs
1970	37.8 yrs	22.3 yrs
1980	38.8 yrs	29.4 yrs

Source: 1990 Statistical Abstract. U.S. Department of Commerce, Washington, D.C.

In 1990, baby boom women ranged in age from 26–44. "Early" female boomers, aged 35 to 44, had a labor force participation rate of 76.5%; for "later" female boomers, aged 25 to 34, the rate was 73.6% (Table 11). These statistics are impressive and clearly demonstrate how the propensity for paid work has led baby boom women to lead very different lives from their mothers and other cohorts of women (Coulson, 1994).

"Later" female boomers have somewhat lower labor force participation rates than their sisters, the "early" boomers, regardless of race (Tables 12 and 16). The reason for this slight difference is attributed to childbearing and child care requirements for "later" female boomers. Baby boom women, while achieving the highest labor force participation rate of any female cohort group, have not reached the levels of employment that baby boom men experience (94.3% vs. 74.9%) (Table 12). For white baby boomers, there is an almost 20-point difference in male and female participation rates; for blacks the spread is smaller, about 14 points. The gender difference among Hispanic baby boomers is more than 30 points.

About one quarter of baby boom women were not in the work force in 1990, a time considered peak productivity years. At the same time, only 5% of baby boom men were not in the work force. This disparity should raise serious doubts concerning assumptions that female retirement will mirror male retirement.

Age

In the past, age was a key predictor of female employment. It appears not to be a factor for baby boom women, indicating a pattern of permanent employment (Coulson, 1994). Historically, women's labor force participation rates by age have resembled an "M" shape, dipping between the early twenties and the main childbearing years of 25 to 34 (Shank, 1988). This reflected the conventional pattern of female employment: young, single women entered the work force, departed upon marriage, remained absent for an extended period for childrearing and family responsibilities or never returned to market work, reentry at mid-life (ages 35–44) and then gradual migration to retirement.

Table 11
Baby Boom Women's Labor Force Participation, 1980–2005

Age	Female Civilian Labor Force (Millions)				Participation Rate (Percent)			
	1980	1990	2000 Proj.	2005 Proj.	1980	1990	2000 Proj.	2005 Proj.
Total	45.5	56.6	66.6	71.8	51.5	57.5	61.6	63.2
16 to	4.4	3.5	4.0	4.2	52.9	51.8	52.0	52.4
20 to	7.3	6.6	6.4	7.2	68.9	71.6	72.5	73.6
25 to	12.3	16.0	14.9	14.8	65.5	73.6	78.1	80.7
35 to	8.6	14.6	18.8	18.6	65.5	76.5	83.0	86.2
45 to	7.0	9.3	14.7	17.4	59.9	71.2	79.7	82.8
55 to	4.7	5.1	6.2	7.8	41.3	45.3	50.3	52.4
65 yrs	1.2	1.5	1.6	1.7	8.1	8.7	8.5	8.8
Age of Baby Boom	16 to 34	26 to 44	36 to 54	41 to 59	16 to 34	26 to 44	36 to 54	41 to 59

Source: 1994 Statistical Abstract No. 615, "Civilian Labor Force and Participation Rates, With Projections: 1970 to 2005." Washington, D.C.: United States Department of Commerce. 1994.

Table 12
Labor Force Participation of Baby Boomers by Age, Sex and Race, 1990

1990	All Baby Boomers		"Late" Baby Boom Men 25–34	"Late" Baby Boom Women 25–34	"Early" Baby Boom Men 35–44	"Early" Baby Boom Women 35–44
	Men	Women				
Total	94.3	74.9	94.2	73.6	94.4	76.5
White	95.3	75.4	95.3	74.2	95.3	76.7
Black	88.4	74.6	88.8	72.3	88.1	77.6
Hispanic	93.6	63.3	94.1	61.4	87.1	66.0

Source: U.S. Department of Labor, Bureau of Labor Statistics, unpublished tabulations from *Current Population Survey,* 1990.

By 1990, baby boom women had changed this long-standing pattern of female participation rates. Baby boom women have generated an inverted "U" shape much like their male counterparts (Figure 6). Two changes occurred: (1) the typical drop off in participation at ages 25 to 34, a decline attributed to women leaving the labor force to have and care for children, disappeared; and (2) the growth in labor force participation of women aged 35–44 (Kutscher, 1993). Table 13 illustrates these changes.

Evidence of the change in employment patterns can be seen as baby boom women reach working age. "Early" female baby boomers (aged 25–34 in 1980) did not follow in the footsteps of their mothers and leave the paid labor force upon marriage or for child care responsibilities. Their younger sisters, the "later" boomers (aged 16–25 in 1980), continued to reverse the pattern. By 1990, the rates for younger female boomers actually rose as they moved from their early to late twenties.

Figure 6
Labor Force Participation Rates, by Age and Sex, Annual Averages, 1948–1994

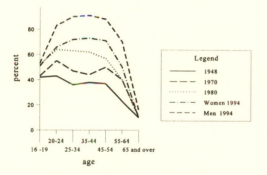

Source: U.S. Department of Labor, Report 892, July, 1995.

Table 13 also illustrates the growth in labor force participation by women in the age group 35–44. By 1990, the net effect of baby boom women's decision to remain in the labor force is that women in their late thirties and early forties have the highest participation rate of any female age group—nearly eight in ten were in the female labor force (U.S. Department of Labor, 1995). The increase in white women's attachment to market work was the cause of this striking statistic.

Table 13
Female Labor Force Participation Rates by Birth Cohort

Year	Participation Rate					
	Age 16–19	Age 20–24	Age 25–34	Age 35–44	Age 45–54	Age 55–64
1960	39.1	46.1	35.8	43.1	49.3	36.7
1970	43.7	57.5	44.8	50.9	54.0	42.5
1980	52.9	68.9	65.5	65.5	59.9	41.3
1990	51.8	71.6	73.6	76.5	71.2	45.3

Source: *1994 Statistical Abstract, 1980 Statistical Abstract*. Washington, D.C.: United States Department of Commerce.

Another significant change that can be attributed to baby boom women's participation rates has been the convergence of the overall age difference between male and female workers (Table 14). For the most part between 1960–1990, the female labor force was younger than the male labor force. The higher participation rates of baby boom women has closed the age gap. By 1995, the median age of the labor force was 37.9 years, with the difference between the female and male median age being minuscule (U.S. Department of Labor, unpublished statistics, 1996). The reason for this convergence is twofold: (1) the higher participation of older baby boom women; and (2) the slowing in participation rate increase of younger women—daughters of baby boom women (Fullerton, 1991).

Today, baby boom women's labor force participation by age approximates the male model of employment—the inverted "U." In addition, any distinction between male and female median ages has disappeared. The social significance of these two demographic changes and it's relevance to the future retirement of baby boom women are:

• First, it confirms that work for baby boom women is no longer a brief episode between school and marriage (U.S. Department of Labor, 1994). The vast majority of baby boom women in the labor market are full-time, career-oriented workers (Shank, 1988). The labor force participation rates by age reflect, for baby boom women, a dramatic change in life cycle status.

• Second, labor force participation rate by age is the demographic variable that has led to the popular, sweeping conclusion that women's employment experience has become very similar to men's. This appears to be true only as it relates to the participation rate by age. As baby boom women's labor force participation rate by age continues to parallel that of baby boom men, the popular tendency to assume that women's life-time work cycle will be a mirror image of men's will lead to false assumptions about future retirement patterns for baby boom women. A deeper examination of the structures of baby boom women's labor force participation (i.e., race, education, marriage, divorce, occupation, patterns of work, earnings) will reveal that their employment is actually more dissimilar than similar to men.

Table 14
Median Ages of the Labor Force, by Sex, Selected Historical Years and Projected Years 1995, 2000, and 2005

	1962	1970	1980	1990	1995	2000	2005
Total	40.5	39.0	34.3	36.6	38.0	39.4	40.6
Men	40.5	39.4	35.1	36.7	38.0	39.4	40.5
Women	40.4	38.3	33.9	36.4	38.0	39.5	40.6

Source: Fullerton, Howard, "Labor Force Projections: The Baby Boom Moves On." *Monthly Labor Review*, November, 1991.

Race

Today, there is slight variation in labor force participation rates between women of different races (U.S. Department of Labor, 1995a). Baby boom women are responsible for changing the racial composition of the female labor force. Historically, clear distinctions in women's labor force participation could be made by race. During the 1960s and 1970s, both black and white women increased their labor force activity even though black female labor force participation has historically been much higher than white women's (U.S. Department of Labor, 1995a). For example, in 1970, the labor force participation rate for married black women with husbands present was 70% compared with 49% for white wives (Fox & Hesse-Biber, 1984). As baby boom women entered the labor market, the gap between black and white women disappeared. By 1990, the rates for black and white women were almost identical—57.8% and 57.5%, respectively (Table 15). White women's participation rate actually exceeded that of black women in 1991. It is projected that by 2005 white women will have the highest labor force participation rates (Fullerton, 1991).

As Table 15 shows, race, in general, plays a minimal role in determining labor force participation for women. This statement holds true for white and black baby boom women, both "early" and "late," but not especially for Hispanic baby boom women (Table 16). White baby boom women (75.4%) are just as likely to be in the labor force as black women (74.6%) but are considerably more likely than Hispanic women (63.3%) (Figure 7).

Table 15
Labor Force Participation Rates of Women, by Race, 1980, 1990, 1991

	1980	1990	1991
All Women	51.5	57.5	57.3
White	51.2	57.5	57.4
Black	53.1	57.8	57.0
Hispanic	47.4	53.0	52.3

Source: U. S. Department of Labor, Bureau of Labor. *Statistics Handbook on Women Workers: Trends & Issues*, Washington, D.C.: 1994.

Table 16
Labor Force Participation of Baby Boomers by Age, Sex and Race, 1990

1990	All Baby Boomers		"Late" Baby Boom Men 25–34	"Late" Baby Boom Women 25–34	"Early" Baby Boom Men 35–44	"Early" Baby Boom Women 35–44
	Men	Women				
Total	94.3	74.9	94.2	73.6	94.4	76.5
White	95.3	75.4	95.3	74.2	95.3	76.7
Black	88.4	74.6	88.8	72.3	88.1	77.6
Hispanic	93.6	63.3	94.1	61.4	87.1	66.0

Source: U.S. Department of Labor, Bureau of Labor Statistics, unpublished tabulations from the *Current Population Survey, 1990*.

During the 1980s, Hispanic women significantly increased their employment; while they accounted for only 7.5% of the total non-institutional population in 1991, they accounted for 12.9% of the increase in total female employment since 1980 (U.S. Department of Labor, 1994). In spite of these increases, Hispanic women have the lowest rates of labor force participation among baby boom women. Higher birth rates, lower educational attainment and cultural attitudes are cited as reasons for this disparity.

Figure 7
Labor Force Participation Rates, by Race, 1990

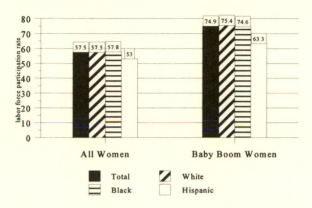

Source: U.S. Department of Labor, Bureau of Labor Statistics, unpublished tabulations from the *Current Population Survey*, 1990 annual averages.

Education

Another distinction of baby boom women is that they are the best educated female cohort group in American history—almost nine of ten baby boom women are high school graduates and nearly one fourth are college educated (Table 17). Baby boom women have strongly invested in their human capital by seeking higher education, once regarded as an opportunity largely available for men. The difference in the proportion of men and women who held college degrees in 1990 declined from a nine percentage point gap for pre-boomers (ages 45–54) to less than four percentage points for baby boomers (ages 25–44) (Bouvier & DeVita, 1991). While a greater proportion (40.7% vs. 37.9 %) of baby boom women completed high school, a greater proportion (27.4% vs. 24.0%) of baby boom men completed college.

Education is an important factor to employment; higher educational attainment produces a greater commitment to the labor force for men and women. The positive influence of education on employment has always existed for women and it is especially true for baby boom women

(Coulson, 1994). Baby boom women's venture in education is reflected in their desire to use their human capital investment in labor market employment. By 1980, all baby boom women were in their early years of labor force participation and their average age was 25 years old. Table 18 shows the percent of life spent economically active by age and sex. This illustrates that as education increases, so does attachment to the paid work force. In 1980, women from age 25 with fifteen years or more of education could expect to spend 51.6% of their lives in paid labor activity, or about forty years of life. Women with less than high school could expect to spend 33% of their lives in paid labor, or about twenty-five years of life. The disparity of educational attainment by baby boom women will certainly impact their retirement experiences. Baby boom women who are better educated will work longer, have shorter retirements, and will have the most financial resources to draw from in retirement.

Table 17
Educational Attainment of Baby Boom Men and Women by Age, 1990

Characteristic	Percent			
	Less Than High School	High School	Some College	College Graduate
All Baby Boomers (25–44)	13.0	39.3	21.9	25.7
ages 25–34	13.7	40.8	21.7	23.7
ages 35–44	12.3	37.6	22.2	27.9
MEN Total (25–44)	13.5	**37.9**	21.2	**27.4**
ages 25–34	14.5	41.0	20.4	24.1
ages 35–44	12.3	34.3	22.2	31.3
WOMEN Total (25–44)	12.6	**40.7**	22.7	**24.0**
ages 25–34	12.9	40.7	23.0	23.3
ages 35–44	12.3	40.7	22.2	24.7

Source: U.S. Department of Labor, Bureau of Labor Statistics, unpublished tabulations from the *Current Population Survey,* 1990 annual averages.

By 1990, labor force participation rates for female baby boomers demonstrated the point that education drives attachment to the labor force (Table 19). "Early" baby boom women with five years or more of college had the highest labor force participation (87.1%); "later" baby boom women with less than four years of high school had the lowest labor force participation (50.2%). The gap continues between male and female participation rates even when education is factored into the equation. While baby boom women have closed the gender gap on educational attainment (Table 17), there is not an equal corresponding gain in labor force participation. For example, the almost twenty-point difference in labor force participation rate between male and female baby boomers drops to only about a fifteen-point difference when college education is factored as a variable. The exception to this is for women with five or more years of college; the difference there is a little less than ten points. While baby boom women have invested significantly in education, the presence of other variables, specifically children, continues to impact female labor force participation. These same variables do not negatively influence their male counterparts.

Marriage, Divorce and Children

In 1990, nearly two-thirds of baby boomers were married, one in eight were divorced, and one in five had never married. Baby boom women were more likely to be married or divorced than baby boom men. One in four baby boom men never married compared with only one in six baby boom women (Bouvier & DeVita, 1991). The baby boom generation created levels of marital instability never seen before. Marriage and divorce are important considerations in analyzing baby boom women because they heavily influence the present and future economic well-being of women (Coulson, 1994).

Figure 8 illustrates the changes in marital status that have occurred between baby boomers and their parents' generation. Baby boomers are much more likely to delay marriage or never marry and divorce more frequently than their parents. Additionally, baby boom married women and mothers are working in the paid labor force much more than their mothers. For the mothers of the baby boom who had a traditional history of market work (periods of market work arranged around family events), retirement was a continuation of their roles as homemakers (Clark, 1989). As discussed in Chapter 3, marriage for the mothers of baby boomers was the best indicator of retirement. Baby boom women, on the other hand, will enter retirement from a dual role model—both as a homemaker and a labor market worker (Coulson, 1994). Marriage will play a much more intricate part in forecasting baby boom women's retirement experience compare to the simplistic role it held for their mothers and grandmothers.

A closer look at the marital status of baby boom women reveals that the majority are married with spouse present (64.8%) (Table 20). In 1990, "later" female baby boomers had a considerably higher percentage of never married (24.4%) compared to their older sisters (9.3%). The reverse, however, is true regarding divorce; "early" female boomers were more likely to be divorced (14.9%) than "later" female boomers (8.8%). These differences can perhaps be attributed to the timing of life cycle events. "Later" female boomers may follow the pattern of their older sisters as they move further into their middle age. However, "early" female baby boomers are expected to have the highest incidence of divorce (Glenn, 1995). Younger boomers may not automatically follow their older sisters on the path to divorce in the same numbers. "Later" boomers are more likely to have experienced divorces of their parents or observed the divorces of older siblings. This may act as a deterrent to marriage or, the opposite, a greater commitment to marriage (Gibson, 1993).

Table 18
Selected Work Life Index by Sex, Race and Educational Attainment, 1979–1980 (for the civilian non-institutional population)

Index and Age	Male					
		Race		Educational Attainment		
	Total	White	Black and Other	Less Than High School	High School to 14 Years	15 Years or More
Percent of life economically active[1]						
From birth	55.4	56.3	50.4	49.4	57.0	58.7
From age 25	70.0	70.6	66.1	61.7	71.5	76.3
From age 60	25.1	25.6	20.0	18.9	26.9	36.0
From age 65	16.2	16.1	13.0	12.7	16.9	25.4
Female						
Percent of life economically active[1]						
From birth	37.9	37.9	37.1	28.7	38.8	46.0
From age 25	44.3	44.1	46.1	33.0	45.0	51.6
From age 60	13.4	13.3	14.3	10.3	14.7	15.6
From age 65	8.1	8.0	8.5	6.5	9.7	9.7

[1]Ratio of Work life expectancy to life expectancy.
Source: U.S. Bureau of Labor Statistics, *Monthly Labor Review*, August, 1985.

Table 19
Labor Force Status of Baby Boom Men and Women and Years of School Completed, 1990—Total, All Races, Labor Force Participation Rate

	Total	<4 Years of High School	4 Years of High School Only	1 to 3 Years of College	4 Years of College or More		
					Total	4 Years Only	5 Years or More
Both sexes							
25–34 yrs	83.7	69.7	83.6	85.9	90.1	90.2	90.0
35–44 yrs	85.2	70.0	84.4	87.6	91.3	89.6	93.4
Women							
25–34 yrs	73.7	50.2	72.4	78.0	84.5	84.0	85.6
35–44 yrs	76.4	55.5	76.6	80.0	83.1	80.0	87.1
Men							
25–34 yrs	94.1	87.8	95.0	95.1	95.7	96.8	93.7
35–44 yrs	94.5	84.9	94.0	95.5	98.1	98.1	98.0

Source: Adapted from U.S. Department of Labor, Bureau of Labor Statistics, unpublished tabulations from the *Current Population Survey,* 1990 annual averages.

Figure 8
Marital Status of Population Ages 25–44, 1960 and 1990

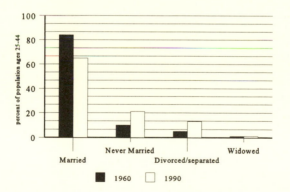

Source: Bouvier & DeVita. "The Baby Boom—Entering Midlife." *Population Bulletin.* 26, no.3 (November, 1991).

Table 20
Marital Status of Baby Boom Females, by Age, 1990

1990	Percent of Total Baby Boom Females	Percent of "Later" Female Baby Boomers (Ages 25–34)	Percent of "Early" Female Baby Boomers (Ages 35–44)
Never Married	17.3	24.4	9.3
Married, Spouse Present	64.8	61.2	69.0
Married, Spouse Absent	5.0	5.0	5.0
Widowed	1.1	0.5	1.8
Divorced	11.7	8.8	14.9

Source: U.S. Department Of Labor, Bureau of Labor Statistics, unpublished tabulations from the *Current Population Survey*, 1990.

Whether baby boom women's entry into market work caused changes in marital status or vice versa, the pattern of baby boom women's labor force participation has narrowed the differences in labor force activity across marital status groups. Historically, never-married and divorced women were those most likely to be employed or looking for work. This pattern continued as the baby boom moved into the labor market. In 1994, 74% of divorced women were in the paid labor force, about the same as in 1972 (72%) (U.S. Department of Labor, 1995a). Substantial differences occurred with married women—in the three decades after World War II, married women more than doubled their participation rate (Shank, 1988). Married women began entering the labor force in increasing numbers in the 1940s (Figure 9). Older married women made up the largest proportion of married women entering the work force during the 1940s, 1950s and 1960s. This began to change in the 1960s, as young married mothers with preschool- or school-age children remained in the labor market. By the 1970s, the majority of women employed, in absolute numbers, were married women (Fox & Hesse-Biber, 1984). By the 1990s, the differences in participation rates by marital groups had narrowed significantly.

In 1990, married women, ages 25 years and older, had a labor force participation rate of 58% (U.S. Department of Commerce, 1994). Baby boom married women had an even greater participation rate of 71.9% (Table 21). "Early" married female boomers have a slightly higher rate in every marital category than their younger sisters (Table 21). Table 21 also illustrates that divorced and never-married baby boom women continue to have the highest labor force participation rates, 84.9% and 81.1% respectively. "Early" baby boom divorced women had the highest participation rate at 86.9%. Female baby boomers who have been divorced, regardless of remarriage, are more likely to be employed than those never divorced (Coulson, 1994). Divorce continues to positively influence women's employment.

Figure 9
Labor Force Participation Rates of Married Women, 1940–1990

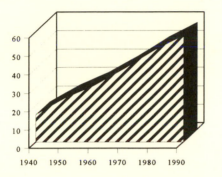

Source: 1994 Statistical Abstract and Fox & Hesse-Biber, 1984.

Table 21
Labor Force Participation Rate of Baby Boom Women by Age and Marital Status, 1990

1990	Total Baby Boom Females	"Later" Female Baby Boomers (Ages 25–34)	"Early" Female Baby Boomers (Ages 35–44)
Never Married	81.1	81.2	81.0
Married, Spouse	71.9	69.8	74.0
Married, Spouse	71.9	70.1	73.9
Widowed	67.7	65.6	68.5
Divorced	84.9	82.0	86.9

Source: U.S. Department of Labor, Bureau of Labor Statistics, unpublished tabulations from the *Current Population Survey,* 1990.

In looking even closer at baby boom women's labor force participation, the greatest increase has occurred among baby boom married women with children. This is an especially important point because while the overall labor force participation numbers for baby boom women look impressive, a deeper investigation of the status of their work—occupation, hours of work, earnings—clearly reveals (aside from age) that their labor force participation does not look like men's. The primary reason for the dissimilarity is children. Children have a negative impact on women's employment; the opposite is true for men. Labor force participation rates reveal very little about actual work experience. For example, in 1992, 73% of the married mothers had work experience but only 37% worked full-time, year-round; 95% of fathers had work experience and 66% worked full-time, year-round (Hayghe & Bianchi, 1994).

By 1990, almost two-thirds of baby boom females had children under the age of 18 and of this group about two-thirds were in the paid labor force. "Early" baby boom mothers (67%) are slightly more likely to combine job and family responsibilities than "later" baby boom working mothers (63%). Delayed marriage and childbearing patterns may explain this difference (Bouvier & DeVita, 1991). It may also explain the notable differences in labor force participation among "early" and "later" baby boom women with children. Figure 10 depicts the distribution of baby boom women in the labor force by age of youngest child. Women with no children (40.5%) is the largest group, followed by women with children aged 6–13. These proportions change significantly when baby boom women are separated into "early" and "later" female boomers in the labor force (Figure 11).

Table 22 and Figure 10 demonstrate that focusing only on the percentage of total baby boom women with children in the labor force will somewhat distort who actually is in the paid labor market. In 1990, the age of female boomers and their life cycle events clearly had an impact on which baby boom women with children were in the labor market (Figure 11). Of the "early" female boomers in the labor force, women with no children (36.1%) and those with children ages 6–13 (34.2%) were most likely to work outside the home; of the "later" female boomers, women with no children (44.6%) and those with children under the age of 3 (20.2%) were most likely to work outside the home. While the proportions differ between the two age groups by age of child, the majority of both "early" and "later" baby boom women with children work. Child care obligations will determine the amount of time the majority of baby boom women will spend working for pay—which will ultimately affect their personal long-term economic outcomes (Hayghe & Bianchi, 1994).

Figure 10
Baby Boom Women in the Labor Force by Age of Youngest Child, 1990

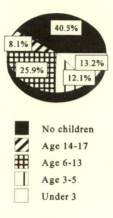

No children
Age 14-17
Age 6-13
Age 3-5
Under 3

Source: U.S. Department of Labor, Bureau of Labor Statistics, unpublished tabulations from the *Current Population Survey*, 1990.

Figure 11
Percentage of Baby Boom Women in the Labor Force by Age and Age of Youngest Child, 1990

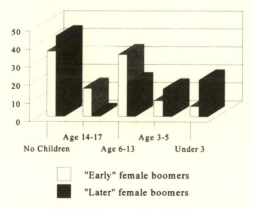

"Early" female boomers
"Later" female boomers

Source: U.S. Department of Labor, Bureau of Labor Statistics, unpublished tabulations from the *Current Population Survey*, 1990.

The presence of children, especially very young children, impacts women's attachment to market work; children have a negative influence on female employment and the younger the child the more negative the effect (Coulson, 1994). Table 23 illustrates how labor force activity rates for mothers fall steadily in line with the age of the youngest child. The participation rates for both "later" (56.9%) and "early" (58.7%) female baby boomers, with own children under age 6, were substantially lower than the overall baby boom female labor force participation rate of 74.9%. This pattern is true for every marital status. Among those with own children under 6, divorced women had the highest labor force participation rates (64.3%; 68.7%), confirming that divorce positively influences female employment. "Later" and "early" mothers with school-age children (6–17) had higher participation rates than mothers of very young children, especially those who were married with spouse present (70.7% and 73.0%, respectively). Also, mothers of school-age children are more likely than those with younger children to work both full-time and year-round outside the home (U.S. Department of Labor, 1995a).

Table 22
Percentage of Baby Boom Women in the Labor Force by Age and by Age of Youngest Child, 1990

1990	Total Baby Boom Females in the Civilian Labor Force		"Later" Female Baby Boomers (Ages 25–34)		"Early" Female Baby Boomers (Ages 35–44)	
	Total No. (1,000)	Percent of Popu- lation	Total No. (1,000)	Percent of Popu- lation	Total No. (1,000)	Percent of Popu- lation
No children	11,746	40.5	6,753	44.6	4,993	36.1
Age 14–17	2,350	8.1	215	1.4	2,135	15.4
Age 6–13	7,526	25.9	2,805	18.5	4,721	34.2
Age 3–5	3,505	12.1	2,306	15.2	1,199	8.7
Under 3	3,832	13.2	3,058	20.2	774	5.6

Source: U.S. Department of Labor, Bureau of Labor Statistics, unpublished tabulations from the *Current Population Survey, 1990.*

Work Status: Full/Part-Time, Hours of Work

More than three-quarters of baby boom women in the labor force in

1990 were employed full-time, that is, 35 hours or more per week, indicating a strong connection to the labor market. Baby boom women's growing attachment to full-time market work resulted in two trends: (1) an increase in full-time, year-round work; and (2) the reduced likelihood of leaving full-time employment. Between 1970–1990, the proportion of women who worked full-time changed very little; what did occur was the shift to full-time, year-round work (U.S. Department of Labor, 1995a). The growth in full-time, year-round employment is a function of women moving from part-time to full-time work and to decreases in the proportion of women leaving full-time employment once they get there (Williams, 1995). Their investment in their own human capital, their career orientation or economic necessity has led baby boom women to move into occupations requiring full-time, year-round schedules.

Closer examination, however, indicates that full-time, year-round work is still not the norm for all baby boom working women. The need for flexible schedules has lead baby boom working mothers, like their mothers before them, to part-time and/or part year work. As Table 23 indicates, both "later" (29.9%) and "early" (33.3%) baby boom women with young children were more likely to work part-time, especially married women (32.3% and 35.9%, respectively).

Table 24 goes into further detail about the actual work experience of baby boom men and women beyond labor force activity rates. It uncovers the differences in work patterns between baby boom men and women and begins to offer a more accurate picture of how much time baby boom women spend at work.

Casual observation of baby boom women's employment would conclude that their labor force participation is similar to men's. However, only 58% of baby boom working women hold full-time, year-round jobs compared to 77% of baby boom men. Baby boom men's work experience is significantly greater than female boomers': they are more likely to work full-time, full-year and have minimal part-time, part-year employment. Only 6% of baby boom men work part-time compared to 23.4% of baby boom women.

Most baby boom women are working full-time, year-round but a significant portion (42%) are employed part-year, full- and part-time (Table 24). "Later" female boomers are the least likely to be employed full-time, year-round (56.9%) and are most likely to work full-time but on part-year status (20.7%). This can be attributed to the fact that, in 1990, "later" female boomers were more likely to have children under age 6 (Table 23). A similar impact on "later" baby boom men's work experience is not evident—73.7% were employed full-time, year-round and only 4% worked part-time, part-year compared to 13% of female "later" boomers.

Table 23
Employment Status of Baby Boom Women by Age, Marital Status and Presence of Children, 1990

	"Later" Female Baby Boomers (Ages 25–34) ""				"Early" Female Baby Boomers (Ages 35–44)			
	Total Emp-loyed (1,000)	LFP %[1]	Full-time[2]	Part-time[3]	Total Emp-loyed (1,000)	LFP %[1]	Full-time[2]	Part-time[3]
All Marital Statuses								
with no children under 18	6,753	84.4	88.1	11.9	4,993	80.2	88.8	11.2
with own children 6 to 17	3,020	69.9	77.2	22.8	6,857	73.9	75.2	24.8
with own children under 6	5,364	56.9	70.1	29.9	1,973	58.7	66.7	33.3
Never Married								
with no children under 18	3,356	85.8	86.8	13.2	1,134	81.3	89.4	10.6
with own children 6 to 17	277	56.9	82.7	17.3	175	69.4	90.3	9.7
with own children under 6	325	43.8	80.9	19.0	61	60.2	85.2	14.8
Married, spouse present								
with no children under 18	2,604	83.7	89.0	11.0	2,415	79.2	85.6	14.4
with own children 6 to 17	1,967	70.7	73.9	26.1	5,229	73.0	71.5	28.5
with own children under 6	4,363	57.8	67.7	32.3	1,694	58.8	64.1	35.9
Married, spouse absent								
with no children under 18	194	73.9	83.5	16.5	225	75.0	91.0	9.0
with own children 6 to 17	228	68.2	82.9	17.1	306	69.2	80.0	20.0
with own children under 6	283	56.0	80.2	19.8	68	47.4	64.7	35.3
Widowed								
with no children under 18	10	53.6	1.00	—	114	77.7	88.6	11.4
with own children 6 to 17	40	84.2	75.0	25.0	88	55.7	72.7	27.3
with own children under 6	35	53.5	57.1	42.9	19	46.2	1.00	—
Divorced								
with no children under 18	588	84.2	92.6	7.4	1,104	82.9	94.6	5.4
with own children 6 to 17	508	75.8	84.0	15.9	1,059	83.9	89.7	10.3
with own children under 6	358	64.3	83.8	16.2	130	68.7	87.7	12.3

[1] Labor force participation rate
[2] Full-time: employed persons on full-time (35 hours or more per week) schedules
[3] Part-time: employed persons on part-time (between 1 and 34 hours per week) schedules
Source: U.S. Department of Labor, Bureau of Labor Statistics, unpublished tabulations from the *Current Population Survey,* 1990.

Table 24
Work Experience of Baby Boom Men and Women by Employment and Age, 1990

Work Experience 1990	Baby Boom Women		Baby Boom Men	
	"Later" (Age 25–34)	"Early" (Age 35–44)	"Later" (Age 25–34)	"Early" (Age 35–44)
Percent of Total who worked	73.6	76.5	94.2	94.4
Percent of Total who worked:				
Full-time[2]	77.6	75.6	93.0	95.0
Part-time[2]	22.4	24.4	7.0	5.0
Percent of Total who:				
Worked **full year** in 1990[1]	**66.2**	**70.7**	**76.6**	**82.4**
Full-time[2]	56.9	59.2	73.7	80.3
Part-time[2]	9.3	11.5	2.9	2.1
Worked **part year** in 1990[3]				
Full-time[2]	**20.7**	**16.4**	**19.3**	**14.7**
40 to 49 weeks	7.8	7.3	9.3	6.6
27 to 39 weeks	4.8	3.7	4.5	3.8
1 to 26 weeks	8.1	5.4	5.5	4.3
Part-time[2]	**13.0**	**12.9**	**4.0**	**2.8**
40 to 49 weeks	3.1	3.7	1.4	0.7
27 to 39 weeks	2.8	3.1	0.8	0.7

[1] Fifty to 52 weeks.
[2] Full-time is defined as 35 hours a week or more. Part-time is less than 35 hours.
[3] One to 49 weeks.
Source: U.S. Department of Labor, Bureau of Labor Statistics, unpublished tabulations from the *Current Population Survey, 1990*; Hayghe, Howard V. and Suzanne M. Bianchi, "Married Mothers' Work Patterns: the Job-Family Compromise." *Monthly Labor Review*, June, 1994.

Figure 12 compares male and female baby boomers work experience. The gender difference in work experience is a function of child care—children negatively impact female employment. In the past, women routinely interrupted their employment to care for children, particularly during the summer months. Taking time out has become less common for baby boom women either because of economic need, fear of wage loss on reentry into the labor force, or occupations requiring them to work year round (U.S. Department of Labor, 1995a; Williams, 1995). Yet, child care remains the responsibility of baby boom women, which is reflected in their patterns of work. This is further accentuated when hours of work are examined. Full-time female boomers work, on average, 41.4 hours per week; baby boom men work, on average, 45.7 hours per week (Bureau of Labor Statistics, unpublished tabulations, 1990). Yet, when hours of work are scrutinized more closely, the gaps between baby boom men and women become clearer.

Figure 12
Baby Boom Work Experience, by Sex, 1990

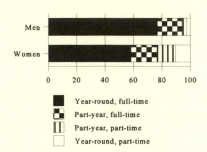

Source: U.S. Department of Labor, Bureau of Labor Statistics, unpublished tabulations from the *Current Population Survey,* 1990.

Figure 13 reveals that differences in hours by gender appear greatest at the extremes. Baby boom women are twice as likely as baby boom men to work less than 35 hours per week; baby boom men are twice as likely as baby boom women to work 49 hours or more a week. Over three-quarters of baby boom working women (79%) with full-time schedules work 40 hours or less a week; almost half of baby boom working men (44%) with full-time schedules work over 40 hours of work per week. More baby boom women are working full-time and year-round schedules, but for the majority of baby boom women their child care and family obligations restrain the number of hours they can work.

Figure 13
Hours of Work for Baby Boom Men and Women, 1990

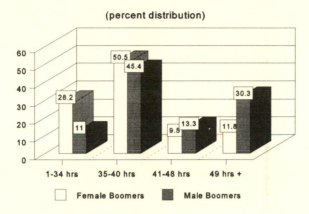

(percent distribution)

Source: U.S. Department of Labor, Bureau of Labor Statistics, unpublished tabulations from the *Current Population Survey,* Annual Averages, 1990.

Occupation

Where baby boom women work further magnifies the differences between male and female baby boom labor force participation. Even though baby boom women have made in-roads into non-traditional jobs—jobs where women constitute 25% or less of the total employed—occupational patterns continue to be segregated by gender. Baby boom women are highly represented in the traditional "female" occupations; baby boom men can be found employed in most all occupational categories but are disproportionately employed in craft and laborer jobs (Table 25). Baby boom women are heavily concentrated in clerical, sales and service jobs in industries that are characterized by part-time and contingent/temporary employment (Table 25) (U.S. Department of Labor, 1995).

Baby boom women are almost exclusively employed in the service sector of our economy—nearly 90% of all baby boom women work in the managerial, professional, technical or service occupations. They are scarcely represented in the manufacturing goods or agriculture sectors of the economy. About one in ten baby boom women work in goods producing jobs and less than one percent can be found in the farming, forestry and fishing industries.

Table 25
**Employment of Baby Boom Men and Women by Major Occupational Group,
1990**

Occupation	Total No. of Baby Boomers Employed (1,000)	Total Baby Boomers Employed, 1990			
		Female		Male	
		Total No.	% of Total	Total No.	% of Total
Total	64,373	29,066	45.2	35,307	54.8
Managerial and professional specialty	18,429	8,794	13.7	9,635	15.0
Executive, administrative, and managerial	8,685	3,675	5.7	5,010	7.9
Professional specialty	9,743	5,119	8.0	4,624	7.1
Technical, sales and administrative support	19,487	12,473	19.4	7,014	10.9
Technicians and related support	2,549	1,278	2.0	1,271	2.0
Sales	6,887	3.097	4.8	3,790	5.9
Administrative support, including clerical	10,051	8.,097	12.6	1,954	3.0
Service	7,298	4,407	6.8	2,891	4.4
Private household	246	237	0.4	9	.01
Protective service	1,164	170	0.2	994	1.5
Service, except private household or protective	5,887	4,000	6.2	1,887	2.9
Precision production, craft, and repair	8,119	679	1.1	7,440	11.6
Operators, fabricators and laborers	9,524	2,456	3.8	7,068	11.0
Machine operators, assemblers, inspectors	4,539	1,756	2.7	2,783	4.3
Transportation/material moving	2,754	256	0.4	2,498	3.9
Handlers, equipment cleaners, helpers, laborers	2,231	445	0.7	1,786	2.8
Farming, forestry and fishing	1,517	258	0.4	1,259	1.9

Source: U.S. Department of Labor, Bureau of Labor Statistics, unpublished tabulations from the *Current Population Survey*, annual averages, 1990. U.S. Department of Labor, Women's Bureau, 1993. *Handbook on Women Workers: Trends & Issues*, 1994.

The greatest proportion of baby boom women (43%) can be found in technical, sales and administrative support jobs—primarily as licensed practical nurses, retail sales workers, cashiers, secretaries, receptionists, bookkeepers and teacher aides. About 20% of baby boom men are found in this occupational category, generally in engineering-related jobs, as sales representatives in insurance, real estate, securities and commodities, and as computer operators. Most of the jobs in this occupational category are skill-based jobs learned either on the job or at a technical or trade school. These jobs do not require extensive investment in human capital and for the most part offer mid- to low earnings potential.

Fourteen percent of baby boom women work in service jobs such as waitresses, cooks, health care aides, maids, hairdressers, and child care workers. These jobs require little or no skill and are compensated accordingly. The nature of these jobs is extremely tenuous; they are characterized by high employee turnover, minimal investment in human capital (either from the individual or the employer), little or no employee benefits and no occupational mobility.

When baby boom women are employed in the goods sector, they tend to be sewing machine operators and factory assemblers. Two percent of baby boom women work in precision production, craft and repair occupations (such as construction trades) and 8% work as operators, fabricators, and laborers. Many of the jobs in these categories require apprenticeship training, ongoing skill development and education. When employers invest heavily in human capital, there is comparable investment in employee compensation and benefits. These jobs tend to offer higher pay, healthcare and pension benefits. Baby boom women have experienced the least job growth in these occupational categories.

Baby boom women have made significant increases in managerial and professional occupations (U.S. Department of Labor, 1995a). Baby boom men (15%) and women (13.7%) are almost equally represented (Table 25). Almost one third of baby boom women work in managerial and professional jobs. The bulk of baby boom women in the professions are found in the financial field as accountants, in the computer world as system analysts and in healthcare as registered nurses. In the management ranks, baby boom women work as financial managers, marketing managers, and school administrators. While the gender gap appears to be shrinking in the managerial and professional occupations, there is evidence that women are more likely than men to be clustered in entry and middle levels of management (U.S. Department of Labor, 1994).

Baby boom women's experience differs from that of baby boom men both in terms of the occupational category and in terms of earnings. This is particularly obvious in the managerial and professional occupations. In 1994, the Women's Bureau of the U.S. Department of Labor reported that more than three-fifths of the occupational classes in which the ratio of women's earnings to men's is 68% or less are in the managerial, professional, and sales categories—areas where baby boom women have experienced the greatest job growth. For example, in 1991, the weekly earnings of women employed as financial managers was 58.7% of what men made in the same occupation; female physicians made 53.9%; female marketing managers made 65.5% (U.S. Department of Labor, 1994). It appears that even among highly paid managers and professionals, the male-female earnings gap continues regardless of identical human capital investment. A 1993 study of University of Michigan Law School graduates demonstrates the impact children and work history have on women's earning potential. A comparison of male and female graduates fifteen years after graduation revealed that the women earned only 60% as much as the male graduates, even though the women started their careers earning only slightly less per year than their male colleagues (Wood, Corcoran & Courant, 1993). The report attributes the earnings gap primarily to women's greater child care responsibilities.

Baby boom women have helped close the occupational gender gap but the gap remains large. The majority of baby boom women occupy traditional "female" jobs. Gender differences in the occupational structure continue to reveal the duality of the labor market. High skill, high paying jobs are the vehicles for occupational and financial advancement. These jobs are found in the managerial and professional specialties, in precision production and as operators and fabricators. Baby boom men are well represented in all these areas—68% of all baby boom men work in these job categories; baby boom women are not nearly as well represented—only 41% can be found working in these occupations. Baby boom women's current earnings and their earnings potential will never equal that of baby boom men because of where they work and the hours they work.

As with the general working population, access to jobs in the primary labor market is unbalanced in favor of the male baby boomer. Only a relatively small portion of baby boom women are found in high skill, high paying jobs. Most baby boom women are employed in the secondary labor market concentrated in low-skill, low-paying jobs with minimal or no pension benefits. In spite of the apparent drawbacks of employment in the secondary labor market, these jobs do offer baby boom women, especially mothers, scheduling flexibility either as part-time or part-year work. Looking at baby boom women's life cycle, their work patterns help solve the family-work pressures in their early and middle adult years, yet it will most likely create or exacerbate problems for them later in life.

Work and Family

The presence of children and educational attainment have the greatest impact on baby boom women's life time earnings potential. For the majority of baby boom women, their labor force participation is shaped by motherhood. The presence of children and their ages determine their probability for labor force employment. Coulson (1994) identified criteria for predicting the labor force participation of a baby boom woman. Using these criteria, Coulson developed an employment model based on a probability formula, which incorporates many of the demographic variables discussed in this chapter. An example of her formula follows:

- For a 35-year-old, married, white baby boom female, who has . . .

    - never divorced
    - a child under 6 years of age
    - 2 years of college
    - a working husband
        . . . the probability of labor market employment is 74.4%.

- If the age of the child was a toddler (less than 3 years of age) but all other variables remained constant, her probability for work outside the home will only be 55.7%.

- If her youngest child was school-aged, her probability would jump to 78.5%.

- If she had graduated from college, her labor force participation rate would rise to 83.4%.

- If she had no other source of household income, the probability of her employment would be 98.5%.

Furthermore, this baby boom woman's hours of work and work status, full- or part-time, part-year or year-round, would be determined by the presence of children and their ages.

The net effect of children on a baby boom woman's labor force participation is ultimately the impact they will have on her earnings potential. Unlike their mothers before them, most baby boom women remained in the labor force upon marriage and during child rearing but with some adjustment to hours of work and work status. The worst-case scenario can be seen for those baby boom women who choose or have chosen to leave the labor market for family reasons and then return once their children reach school age. Gaps in employment are extremely costly to baby boom women. The following hypothetical situation is presented to illustrate the extent child rearing has on baby boom women's labor force participation and life time earnings:

- A baby boom woman born in 1952:
    - graduates from college in 1973
    - immediately goes to work full-time and year-round
    - works in financial services in Chicago
    - marries and at age 25 leaves paid work for seven years to care for her child
    - returns to full-time employment in 1984 at age 32.

- It is estimated that this seven-year employment gap will cost this baby boom woman the equivalent of ten years of earnings. Even if she stays in the paid labor force for twenty more years, she will still earn between 5–7% less than her peers who never left the labor force (Jacobsen & Levin, 1995).

Employers view employment gaps as an indication of weak attachment to paid labor. Lost seniority, lost on-the-job training opportunities, skill depreciation or obsolescence, lost networking connections and wage differentials are the costs of intermittent labor force attachment (Felmlee, 1995). It is unknown how many baby boom women have opted to leave the paid labor force for family reasons. However, it can be inferred that for at least two-thirds of baby boom women, at some time during their working life, they will terminate and/or reduce attachment to the paid labor force to care for children, or as they age, to provide elder care. This dynamic within baby boom women's work is not experienced by baby boom men. Intermittent labor force attachment continues the earning differentials between female and male baby boomers. The cumulative effect of female boomers' work patterns will impact their pension incomes, Social Security earnings, and personal savings—the financial foundations of retirement.

Baby boom women will continue increasing their labor force participation rates as they move through their peak productivity years. Current projections indicate that by the year 2005, "early" female baby boomers will begin to drop out of the labor force as they move closer to the traditional retirement and early retirement ages; "later" female boomers will maintain a high participation rate (Table 26). Whether "early" female baby boomers begin to follow past retirement patterns is a precarious assumption. Baby boom women's attachment to the paid labor force, the long-term impact of divorce, the presence of dependent children, continuing financial obligations, etc., may prove strong enough to slow the pattern of early retirement.

Table 26
Baby Boom Women's Labor Force Participation, 1980–2005

Age	Female Civilian Labor Force (Millions)				Participation Rate (Percent)			
	1980	1990	2000 Proj.	2005 Proj.	1980	1990	2000 Proj.	2005 Proj.
Total	45.5	56.6	66.6	71.8	51.5	57.5	61.6	63.2
16 to 19	4.4	3.5	4.0	4.2	52.9	51.8	52.0	52.4
20 to 24	7.3	6.6	6.4	7.2	68.9	71.6	72.5	73.6
25 to 34	12.3	16.0	14.9	14.8	65.5	73.6	78.1	80.7
35 to 44	8.6	14.6	18.8	18.6	65.5	76.5	83.0	86.2
45 to 54	7.0	9.3	14.7	17.4	59.9	71.2	79.7	82.8
55 to 64	4.7	5.1	6.2	7.8	41.3	45.3	50.3	52.4
65 yrs +	1.2	1.5	1.6	1.7	8.1	8.7	8.5	8.8
Age of Baby Boom Women	16 to 34	26 to 44	36 to 54	41 to 59	16 to 34	26 to 44	36 to 54	41 to 59

Source: *1994 Statistical Abstract, No. 615*, "Civilian Labor Force and Participation Rates," with Projections: 1970 to 2005.

SUMMARY

The nature of work for baby boom women is different from that of baby boom men. Shared assumptions about retirement are not realistic, given the gender differences in baby boom labor force participation. Even among baby boom women, labor force participation, work patterns and demographics have created diverse working lives that make it a challenge to predict future retirement behavior. Their demographic profiles—their age, race, education, marital status, children—define their place in the working world. Baby boom women joined the paid labor force by choice *and* necessity (Coulson, 1994). It is therefore assumed that these same variables will help define their retirement experience.

Baby boom women's work patterns (full- and part-time, part-year, year-round status and hours of work), while moving closer to the male model of labor force participation, remain substantially different from that of baby boom men. Gender differences in baby boom work patterns should raise "red flags" regarding their future retirement and any assumptions that baby boom women's retirement will resemble men's retirement. Baby boom women's attachment to part-time, part-year work is of concern due to the increasingly involuntary nature of that type of employment, low wages and lack of health and pension benefits. Hours of work also have bearing on current earnings and benefits, which ultimately influence future retirement income.

Baby boom women have developed strong ties to the labor market that tolerate the pressures of marriage and child care. They have helped make it culturally acceptable for mothers to be breadwinners as well as caregivers, albeit, with some cost to their own personal economic future. Baby boom women have dramatically changed the composition of the labor force, specifically, the female labor force. They have brought about an age and race convergence, the dual-earner married couple, working mothers, and career women and mothers. On their road to permanent employment they have made female labor force participation more diverse and less predictable. However, one variable that has remained unchanged is the role children play in defining women's paid employment. Women remain the primary caretakers of children and their labor force participation reflects this responsibility.

5

Retirement Income for Women

The financial status of baby boom women will be the culmination of a life time of personal and economic decisions. Decisions about education, marriage, childbearing and labor force participation will all determine a financial outcome relevant for their retirement experience. This chapter will examine the economic conditions impacting baby boom retirement income, how baby boom women will fare financially in retirement and what, if anything, baby boom women are currently doing to prepare and plan for their retirement years.

The sources of retirement income for today's elderly (Figure 14) will be the same for the baby boom. Today's retirees receive 40% of their income from Social Security payments, 21% from asset income (primarily home ownership), 19% from pension income (public and private) and 17% from earnings. Unknown for the baby boom is what mix of income sources—Social Security, pensions, assets and earnings—will most likely provide secure retirement. These sources of income will be examined to identify how baby boom women will pay for their retirement. Throughout this examination, comparisons to current female retirees and to baby boom men will be made to illustrate similarities and differences between the mothers of baby boom women and their male counterparts.

In any discussion of the future financial status of women, it is imperative to reflect on the social meaning of retirement. Retirement is an "earned" benefit; it is an entitlement based on the concept that hard work during early and middle adult years will produce a comfortable life upon retirement from paid work. Baby boom women will be the first generation of women who will earn Social Security benefits as workers, not as spouses. Social Security entitlements are paid as worker benefits, spousal benefits or dual entitlement benefits; worker benefits are based on a woman's own earnings record while spousal and dual entitlement benefits hinge on the earnings of her husband. Female labor force participation patterns for prior cohorts of women have precluded them from receiving worker benefits; rather, their Social Security receipts were based on their spouses' earnings. While earning Social Security worker benefits may be an historic first for women, it does not necessarily bode well for baby boom women. This notion of "earned" is critical to understanding why a generation of women, who have spent their adult years in the paid labor force, will not be as entitled as their male counterparts. The reason for this is the social-contextual differences in baby boom women's work-life experiences and their labor force participation patterns. Retirement, defined as no longer engaging in paid labor, may not be possible for some women, particularly working-class women and women of color (Calasanti & Bonanno, 1992). Baby boom women's labor force participation patterns (as discussed in Chapter 4) make them vulnerable to economic losses associated with retirement (Hatch & Thompson, 1992). Women earn less than men and baby boom women's attachment to their spouses' earnings has eroded, primarily due to divorce. Unless the notion of "earned" is changed, baby boom women will not be as entitled to retirement benefits as their male counterparts.

Figure 14
Sources of Income for the Aged

Source: AARP and the Administration on Aging. *A Profile of Older Americans.* Washington, D.C.: 1995. Pamphlet.

THE BABY BOOM'S FINANCIAL FUTURE

Baby boomers have been big spenders, not savers. However, the question as to whether the parents of baby boomers were more fiscally responsible is not at issue. Baby boomers and other American generations have done a relatively poor job of saving for retirement. In fact, cross-generational studies seem to show that baby boomers have managed to acquire more wealth than their parents had at the same ages (Cantor & Yuengert, 1994; Manchester, 1993). The baby boom's parents are relatively well off because of well-funded company pension plans, indexed Social Security benefits during the 1970s and the real estate boom of the 1970s and 1980s (Bernheim, 1993a). Boomers have and will face very different and less advantageous economic and social conditions. The degree to which these conditions influence the financial future of the baby boom sets the parameters of the debate.

There are conflicting views in the literature about the financial future of the baby boom. The prevailing position foretells tough economic times in retirement; others see baby boomers entering retirement in better financial shape than their parents. Agreement does exist, however, on the economic climate that baby boomers have experienced while growing up. The baby boom's labor force years have been plagued by slowed economic growth, increased inequality in the distribution of income and little or no wage growth (Kingson, 1991; Easterlin, MacDonald & Macunovich, 1990). The law of supply and demand hurt the baby boom during their entry and tenure in the job market; it may also work against baby boomers in retirement (Easterlin, Schaeffer & Macunovich, 1993; Greenwald, 1989). The diversity of the baby boom generation and income polarization, which will continue as the cohort ages, compound efforts at generalizing about the financial future of this cohort.

Easterlin represents the most optimistic voice of the future of baby boom retirement. His research (1993) contends that, on average, boomers' economic status is considerably better than their parents' at the same point in the life cycle and will most likely continue into retirement. His conclusion is based on income and wealth comparisons. Table 27 indicates that "early" baby boomers (1945–54) more than doubled ($52,800) the net worth of their parents ($24,636) at the same time period in their life cycle (age 35–44).

Easterlin argues that the baby boom has adapted to the social and economic challenges by having fewer children, greater numbers remaining single, and sending married women into the paid labor market, even during child rearing years. He cites an exception to his positive outlook—the poorest segment of the boomers, especially poor "later" boomers, will not share in the retirement security he predicts for the majority of baby boomers.

Table 27
Median Net Worth at Age 35–44, Specified by Birth Cohort

Birth Cohort	Year in Which Cohort is Age 35–44	Net Worth (1989 Dollars)
1909–18	1953	20,806
1918–27	1962	24,636
1939–48	1983	49,800
1945–54	1989	52,800

Source: Esterlin, Richard, Christine M. Schaeffer, Dianne J. Macunovich, "Will the Baby Boomers Be Less Well Off Than Their Parents?" *Population and Development Review*, 19, no. 3 (September, 1993).

Other researchers support Easterlin's positive position and predict a secure financial future. Andrews and Chollet's (1988) analysis of the retirement income prospects of the baby boom finds any dire predictions unwarranted. Using the Pension and Retirement Income Simulation Model (PRISM), they found that average Social Security income is projected to rise, largely due to greater rates of labor force participation by baby boom women and rising real wage growth. Partial findings are illustrated in Table 28. Andrews and Chollet estimate that 97% of baby boom retired families (married couples and single retirees) will receive Social Security income. Seventy-one percent would receive employer-sponsored pensions. The authors presume that the baby boom will "reap the fruits of a mature employer-sponsored pensions system." This assumption may prove too optimistic given the shifts in the labor market and pension coverage that have occurred since this report was published (1988).

Like Easterlin, Andrews and Chollet contend that, on average, the baby boom will retire under favorable financial circumstances with the exception of one group—baby boom women who are single at retirement. The PRISM projections in their study indicate that 97% of baby boom women who are single at retirement will have Social Security benefits. A cursory look at this statistic could lead to the conclusion that single baby boom women, at retirement, will be better off than current retiring single female cohorts. The authors caution against such a conclusion emphasizing that poverty is an enduring problem for single elderly women regardless of work history. Table 29 reveals that, in 1988, 65% of current single female retirees were in or near poverty; at the time of their retirement, nearly half (43.3%) of single baby boom women are expected to be in or near poverty. The authors project that the average retirement income among single baby boom women will be significantly less than that of couples or single men. Married baby boom men and women are the least likely to be in poverty or near poverty (1.6%). Baby boom women's labor force participation will reduce, somewhat, the likelihood of poverty for single women at retirement. However, longer work histories will not eradicate the risk of poverty for single women in their old age.

Table 28
Percent of Retired Families of Different Generations with Retirement Income at Age 67 from Various Sources

Income Source	Workers Currently Retiring[a]	Baby Boom Retirees[b]
All Retiree Families		
Social Security	86	97
Employer-sponsored pensions	48	71
Earnings	35	29
Supplemental Security Income	10	3
Married Couples		
Social Security	94	98
Employer-sponsored pensions	59	83
Earnings	44	39
Supplemental Security Income	2	–
Single Individuals		
Social Security	77	95
Employer-sponsored pensions	36	60
Earnings	25	21
Supplemental Security Income	21	5

Note: Based on data from Employee Benefit Research Institute tabulations of the Pensions and Retirement Income Simulation Model (PRISM), 1986.
[a] Age 55–64 in 1979.
[b] Age 25–34 in 1979.
Source: Andrews, Emily and Deborah J. Chollet, *Future Sources of Retirement Income: Whither the Baby Boom.* Lexington, MA: 1988.

A 1993 report by the Congressional Budget Office essentially replicates the position taken by Easterlin and others (Manchester, 1993). Four primary reasons for a bright financial future are offered:

- boomers will have higher real pre-retirement earnings if real wage growth is positive over the next 20–40 years;

- baby boom women's increased eligibility for Social Security and pension benefits due to their labor force participation;

- boomers will more likely receive pension income as a result of recent changes in pension laws;

- boomers may inherit substantial wealth from their parents.

Table 29
Percent of Retirees of Different Generations in Poverty or Near Poverty[a] at Age 67, by Sex and Marital Status at Retirement

	Workers Currently Retiring[b]	Baby Boom Retirees[c]
All Individuals	25.1	18.6
Married men and women	11.2	1.6
Single men	31.5	5.4
Single women	64.9	43.3

Note: Based on data from Employee Benefit Research Institute tabulations of the Pensions and Retirement Income Simulation Model (PRISM), 1986.
[a] Retirees with family/personal income equal to 125% of poverty or less.
[b] Age 55–64 in 1979.
[c] Age 25–34 in 1979.
Source: Andrews, Emily and Deborah J. Chollet, *Future Sources of Retirement Income: Whither the Baby Boom.* Lexington, MA: 1988.

The study declares that most baby boomers will enjoy higher incomes and more wealth than their parents. However, it also identifies exceptions to this bright financial future. Baby boomers without marketable job skills, single boomers, and non-home owners risk a bleaker economic future. The absence of one or all three indicators—education, marriage, and home ownership—could seriously skew chances of a secure retirement. College-educated boomers can expect higher incomes, faster wage growth, and more savings resources. Marriage offers shared expenses, especially housing, increased savings opportunities, and fringe benefits such as health insurance coverage. Finally, capital gains on housing assets, have, at least in the past, increased wealth.

The biggest critic of the optimistic forecast is Douglas Bernheim, a Princeton University economics professor. Bernheim (1993a) suggests that most researchers are asking the wrong question. Rather than asking if baby boomers will be as well off as their parents, the critical question is whether baby boomers will be able to sustain their standard of living in retirement. Bernheim contends that the current generation of retirees was extraordinarily lucky. The parents of baby boomers were recipients of good fortune when they reached old age—housing prices skyrocketed, public and private retirement benefits rose significantly and high inflation eroded the real value of their debts (e.g., fixed-rate mortgages).

Bernheim led the highly publicized (1993a) Merrill Lynch study, "Is the Baby Boom Generation Preparing Adequately for Retirement?" which contradicted the Congressional Budget Office report cited above. The Merrill Lynch report estimated that baby boomers must triple their current rate of savings to avoid a sudden drop in living standard upon retirement. The report further warns that baby boom women will need more savings than baby boom men since they will work fewer years and earn less. Baby boomers cannot expect to be as lucky as their parents. Bernheim recommends increased savings and financial planning if baby boomers seek to achieve a secure retirement.

Advocates of the pessimistic outlook argue that the baby boom's sources of retirement income have been and will continue to be much affected by economic and social changes and trends:

- Social Security will be scaled back. Social Security is by far the most important source of income for today's retirees. Ninety percent of the elderly receive it (Rix, 1993). Baby boomers will also receive Social Security but are likely to receive much smaller Social Security checks in old age. They will also most likely pay more taxes on those checks than do today's elderly (Anand, 1993).

- Two trends have been occurring with pension coverage. The first is that cost-conscious employers are shifting the burden of saving for retirement to the individual employee. The second is that there has been ongoing stagnation and even a slight decline in private pension expansion (Rix, 1993; Dennis & Axel, 1991; Piacentini, 1989).

- Housing values are likely to rise no faster than inflation, making home ownership less attractive as a savings vehicle for the baby boom. Baby boomers should not count on rapidly rising home values to finance their retirement as their parents did.

- The baby boom's life choices have commingled many early-life activities with traditional later-life issues. Day-care costs, college costs, and care for elderly parents will make saving difficult for baby boomers.

- Inheritance may not be the major source of income many boomers expect. A recent study by Cornell University predicts that baby boomers will receive the largest pool of inheritance ever in the United States, over $11 trillion. However, about two thirds of this inheritance is likely to be concentrated in the hands of about 10% of the boomers (Krysty, 1995). According to the Congressional Budget Office, the *median* inheritance is only $30,000 per person—the cost of one year in a nursing home for mom or dad (O'Reilly, 1995).

While both camps argue passionately about the financial future of the baby boom, it is prudent to note who is saying what. Both sides are attempting to influence public policy and vested interests are at play. This dynamic within the debate has great bearing on how the data are interpreted. For example, Russell (1995) points out that the Merrill Lynch calculations do not include housing wealth, the baby boomer's most important financial asset. The Employee Benefit Research Institute (EBRI) maintains that if housing is entered into the equation, baby boomers are saving at 84% of the rate needed to maintain their standard of living in retirement.

The majority of "doomsayers" come from the ranks of economists, benefits consultants, pension experts and financial services companies such as Merrill Lynch. Their message is most often heard in the mass media. On the other hand, the biggest champion of the "bright future" scenario is the U.S. Government. Forces of bureaucracy (and it's inherent inertia) may be at work here to continue current retirement policies and practices.

A strong case can be made for a positive financial future for the baby boom generation. The retirement security of a majority of baby boomers is all but certain. However, a strong case can be made that the retirement years for many boomers—such as the currently poor, single parents, low-wage workers, non-home owners—will likely be bleak. While their exact numbers cannot be estimated, they will be found disproportionately among the roughly 14 million households headed by female baby boomers in 1990.

SOURCES OF RETIREMENT INCOME

Forecasts of the retirement income of the baby boom have been made over the past few years using PRISM simulations and Current Population Survey data (e.g., AARP's 1994 Aging Baby Boomers report, Congressional Budget Office's 1993 paper, Andrews & Chollet's 1988 study). As Figure 15 illustrates, the sources of retirement income for baby boomers will be very similar to their parents' generation. Social Security will provide the largest share of income for baby boomers

(38%), as it does for their parents today (40%). It is expected that Social Security will decline in relative importance as pension receipts increase for baby boomers (24%).

Figure 15
Sources of Retirement Income for Baby Boomers (2030) and Their Parents (1992)

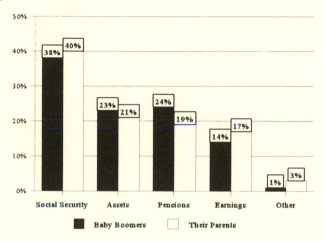

Note: These comparisons are based on actual and projected aggregate income among persons ages 66–84 in 1992 and baby boomers in 2030.
Source: American Association of Retired Persons and the Administration on Aging. Adapted from *Aging Baby Boomers: How Secure Is Their Future?* Washington, D.C.: 1994.

Changes in vesting schedules and baby boom women's increased labor force participation will make many more baby boomers eligible for pension income. A cautionary note needs to be added, however, since the benefit levels for baby boomers will be fairly low compared to current retirees. Asset income will be somewhat larger (23%) for baby boomers but will be concentrated among those with higher incomes (AARP, 1994). Finally, it is anticipated that earnings income will be actually lower for baby boomers (14%) than it is today for their parents (17%). It is assumed that the baby boom will take early retirement and the labor force participation rates of the elderly will continue to decline (AARP, 1994; Manchester, 1993; Andrews & Chollet, 1988).

Table 30 confirms the above discussion by looking at the percentage of persons receiving each income source and comparing the forecast for baby boomers with their parent's generation. It is forecasted that most all baby boomers will have Social Security income (98%) and some form of asset income (90%). The greatest projected change between baby boomers and their parents is pension income, 82% compared to 50%.

Table 30
Percent Receiving Income Sources—Comparison of Baby Boomers (2030) with Today's Elderly (1990)

Sources of Income	1990 (Elderly Persons Age 66–84)	2030 (Projected)
Social Security	93%	98%
Assets	72%	90%
Pensions	50%	82%
Earnings	22%	17%

Source: American Association of Retired Persons. Adapted from *Aging Baby Boomers: How Secure Is Their Economic Future?* Washington, D.C.: 1994. Booklet.

The financial security of the baby boom's retirement hinges on the assumption that baby boomers will have three sources from which to draw retirement income—Social Security, assets, and pensions. The "bright future" painted for the baby boom is for those boomers with all three sources of retirement income. Projections indicate that nearly three quarters of boomers will have access to all three sources (Table 31). It is further projected that the median income ($32,900), in 1990 dollars, of boomers with all three sources will be about 80% higher than the median income ($18,400) for those with two sources (AARP, 1994). Median income for boomers with only one source will be about $10,000. Of all baby boomers, those who are married and college-educated with high incomes will be the group most likely to have access to all three retirement sources; those least likely will be single females with a high school education or less who are poor or near poor (Table 31).

Hard data seems to bear out that baby boomers, on average, will be better prepared financially for retirement than the "doomsayers" are predicting (Russell, 1995). The "appearance" of these data may lead to the conclusion that the financial future of baby boom women looks promising, especially given their labor force participation rates. The face value assumptions of this conclusion need to be challenged since structural inequities exist for women in the labor market (see Chapter 4).

Table 31
Characteristics of Baby Boomers by Number of Sources of Income from Social Security, Pensions and Assets in 2030

Characteristics	Boomers with Three Sources	Boomers with Two Sources	Boomers with One Source
Total Baby Boom	73.7%	22.9%	3.4%
Gender			
Male	77.7	20.0	2.3
Female	70.3	25.3	4.2
Marital Status			
Married	82.8	16.2	1.0
Single	61.4	31.8	6.5
Widowed	69.4	26.1	4.6
Education Level			
Less than High School	69.8	25.3	4.6
High School Graduate	70.9	24.5	4.6
Some College	74.9	22.1	2.7
Economic Status			
Poor or Near Poor	29.5	50.7	19.4
Moderate Income	58.3	36.2	5.6
Moderate to High Income	78.7	20.1	0.7

Note: Totals may not always add to 100% because some boomers in different groups will have no income from any of these three sources in 2030.
Source: American Association of Retired Persons. Adapted from *Aging Baby Boomers: How Secure Is Their Economic Future?* Washington, D.C.: 1994. Booklet.

The key will be to question the "on average" preface stipulated in the economic projections. Labor market inequities will translate into future retirement income patterns for many baby boom women that may not be "on average." Baby boom women face a different financial future than their male counterparts since they:

• will have fewer years in the labor force; an average of 29.4 years compared to 38.8 years for baby boom men (see Chapter 4);

• experience more interrupted work histories; women move in and out of the labor force with greater frequency than men, spend longer periods of time away from paid work and change jobs more often (Talaga & Beehr, 1995; Rix, 1993); women average 11.5 years away from the labor force, while men average 1.3 years (U.S. Senate Select Committee on Aging, 1991);

• are more concentrated in low-wage occupations; about 60% of baby boom women work in clerical, sales, and service jobs (see Chapter 4);

- are less likely to work in industries with pension coverage; they will receive lower Social Security benefits than baby boom men; they will qualify less often for private pension benefits and get less in the way of private pension benefits when they do qualify (Talaga & Beehr, 1995; Rix, 1993);

- will accumulate less in the way of assets and savings by the time they reach retirement age (Talaga & Beehr, 1995; Rix, 1993).

Female boomers are as demographically diverse as the entire baby boom generation, which is to say that the "bright future" predicted for the cohort may be enjoyed by many baby boom women but, most likely, will not be by many others. To form a more accurate picture of retirement income for women, a deeper examination into each income source is needed.

Social Security Income for Baby Boom Women

The literature is clear about the treatment of women in the U.S. Social Security system. America's retirement system is gender neutral; it is the interaction of life time earnings patterns with the system's provisions that results in differences between men and women (Ross & Upp, 1993; United States House of Representatives, Select Committee on Aging, 1992). Social Security is a "pay as you go" system and benefits are based on earnings. For women, this is the crux of the matter. Benefits are tabulated on length of time in paid labor and the amount of wages earned over a life time.

In 1983, Congress enacted a delay in the "normal" age for Social Security eligibility, which makes normal retirement age 66 years old for the "early" boomers and 67 years old for "later" boomers (Crystal, 1988). Baby boom women will qualify for Social Security benefits in one of three ways—worker benefits, spousal benefits or dual entitlement benefits.

Worker Benefits. Worker benefits are received as entitlement solely as a retired or disabled worker based on a woman's own earnings. Worker benefits are determined by a worker's primary insurance amount (PIA). PIA is calculated based on earnings over a period of 40 years, from which the five years of lowest earnings are deducted. Those five years may actually be years of no earnings (Rix, 1993). If a woman has spent more than five years in unpaid labor activities (e.g., caregiving, homemaking, etc.), those years are reflected as zero earnings years. These zero earnings years are also calculated into annual earnings to produce a worker's average life time earnings.   The impact of zero earnings years will be significant for baby boom women even though they will spend most of their adult years in the paid labor market. The Urban Institute's Center for Women Policy Studies (1988) estimated that by the time "early" female boomers begin to retire, around 2010, only about 22% will suffer no effects from zero averaging (Figure 16). By 2030, when all female boomers will have reached age 65, less than four in ten women age 62–69 will have worked 35 years or more. The remaining 60% will have some zero averaging in their earnings records. Under current Social Security provisions, it appears that only a little more than a third of baby boom women will earn the right to maximize their Social Security earnings.

Figure 16
Women Will Spend More Years in the Labor Force But Many Will Still Be "Zeroed" Out

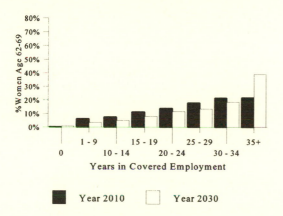

Source: Urban Institute. *Earnings Sharing in Social Security: A Model for Reform.* Washington, D.C.: Center for Women Policy Studies, 1988, p.21.

In 1994, women's wages were 76% of men's wages (U.S. Department of Labor, 1995a). Baby boom women's entry and participation in the labor market has substantially narrowed the gap between men's and women's earnings (Table 32). The shrinking of earnings differentials is attributed to the educational attainment of baby boom women. It may be logical to assume that since baby boom women's labor force participation has narrowed the earnings gap, it should also narrow the gap in Social Security benefits between men and women. If what has occurred with current retirees is any indication, that assumption is incorrect. In 1970, women's average Social Security benefits were 78% of men's; in 1995, the percentage dropped to 76%, even though retired women worked more years than their mothers (Older Women's League, 1995). Between 1960 and 1989, the number of women of all ages who were eligible based on their own work records increased from 27.5 million to 74.1 million (Lingg, 1990). Despite this tremendous increase, it appears that women may earn less from their own paid labor than they would receive in retirement from their spouses' earnings. It must be assumed that the earnings gap will continue until and during retirement regardless of the progress baby boom women have made in the labor market. This gap is a function of total years of employment, occupational differences, and variations in hours of work (see Chapter 4) intersecting with the provisions of Social Security. The nature of work for baby boom women, offset as it is by social and family responsibilities, ultimately lowers their Social Security "worker" benefits.

Spousal Benefits. Spousal benefits are an entitlement received solely as a wife or widow based on her husband's earnings record; she would receive an amount equal to half her husband's benefit and after he dies, a benefit equal to his retirement benefit. Spousal benefits will be available for those few baby boom women who do not accumulate the requisite number of quarters of coverage required for worker benefits. In 1960, 57% of women were entitled solely as a wife or widow while 43% received worker benefits. By 1988, the numbers had almost reversed—40% were entitled solely as wives or widows and 60% were entitled as workers (Lingg, 1990). Entitlement solely as a wife or widow will continue to decline given baby boom women's labor force participation. The importance of this entitlement for baby boom women will be eligibility for dual entitlement.

Dual Entitlement Benefits. Dual entitlement benefits are an entitlement based on a woman's own earnings and those of her husband because the amount of her worker benefit is less than her benefit as a wife or widow; she will receive an amount equal to the higher of the two benefits. Dual entitlement is a woman's benefit, a potentially dubious benefit for some women (Ross & Upp, 1993). In 1990, 4.7 million women were dually entitled compared to about 100,000 men (United States House of Representatives, Select Committee on Aging, 1992). The percentage of women receiving Social Security benefits based on their own work records has remained quite constant since 1960 (Table 33) even with women, especially married women, entering the labor force in large numbers.

Table 32
Median Weekly Earnings of Full-Time Wage and Salary Workers by Sex, 1979–1994 Annual Earnings (In Current and Constant [1994] Dollars)

Years	Median earnings		Ratio of Women's to Men's Earnings
	Men	Women	
	Current Dollars		
1979	$291	$182	62.5
1980	312	201	64.4
1981	339	219	64.6
1982	364	238	65.4
1983	378	252	66.7
1984	391	265	67.8
1985	406	277	68.2
1986	419	290	69.2
1987	433	303	70.0
1988	449	315	70.2
1989	468	328	70.1
1990	485	348	71.8
1991	497	368	74.0
1992	505	381	75.4
1993	514	395	76.8
1994	522	399	76.4
	Constant (1994) Dollars		
1979	$594	$372	62.6
1994	522	399	76.4
Percent change	-12.1	7.3	—

Source: U.S. Department of Labor. *Women in the Workforce: An Overview,* Report 892, Washington, D.C.: July, 1995.

In 1960, about 39% of women received "worker" benefits; by 1988, the proportion had changed little—to 38%. However, the number of women who are dually entitled has grown significantly, from 4.5% in 1960 to 22% in 1988. This percentage rose even further, to 25%, by 1993 while entitlement based solely on women's own work records remained almost constant at 36% (Older Women's League, 1995).

Table 33
Women Beneficiaries Aged 62 and Older, by Type of Entitlement, 1960–1988 (in Percentage)

Benefit Type	1960	1970	1980	1988
Worker only	38.8	42.1	41.1	37.6
Dual Entitlement	4.5	8.5	15.8	22.0
Spousal Only	56.7	49.4	43.1	40.3

Note: Percentages are based on all women 62 and older who were receiving benefits.
Source: Adapted from B.A. Lingg, "Women Beneficiaries Aged 62 or Older, 1960–88." *Social Security Bulletin,* 53, no. 7, (July, 1990).

When a woman is dually entitled, it means that her spousal benefit is higher than her retired worker benefit. The irony of the dual entitlement provision is that while working women pay payroll taxes for many years (reducing their disposable income) they do so for no additional benefits (United States House of Representatives, Select Committee on Aging, 1992). It is highly likely that a woman with years of paid work experience would be entitled to higher Social Security benefits as the spouse of a retired worker than as a retired worker herself. A married woman who earns income and contributes to the system may not receive benefits any greater than if she had chosen not to work. Furthermore, because the Social Security system was created on the life-long breadwinner (male) model, a two-earner couple making the same income as a one-earner couple can end up paying thousands more in taxes for no increase in benefits (Table 34).

Much has been written about the frailties and weaknesses of the Social Security system, especially for women. Ross and Upp (1993) conclude that the Social Security reforms needed to reflect the demographic, economic, and social changes affecting American families and women: (1) will cost more than current policymakers are willing to pay; and (2) society is unlikely to abandon the traditional principles embodied in the present system. Therefore, the reality for married and divorced baby boom women is that many may retire as dually entitled. Also, it is very likely that baby boom women will contribute more in payroll taxes but actually get less in their old age than their mothers (who most likely did not work outside the home). The reason for this is not only the dual entitlement scenario, but the increases in the payroll tax rate and the taxable wage base over the past 25 years.

Table 34
1992 Earnings and Contributions and Monthly Social Security Benefits (in 1992 Dollars) for Workers Retiring in 2010[a]

		Abbotts	Costellos
Earnings			
	Husband	$70,000	$50,000
	Wife	$0	$20,000
Family Total		$70,000	$70,000
Contributions (OASDI)[b]			
	Husband		
	Employer	$3,441	$3,100
	Worker	$3,441	$3,100
	Wife		
	Employer	$0	$1,240
	Worker	$0	$1,240
Family Total		**$6,882**	**$8,880**
Benefits			
	Husband	$1,420 WB[c]	$1,420 WB
	Wife	$710 SB[c]	$710 SB
Family Total		**$2,130**	**$2,130**

[a] Benefits are for workers retiring at age 66 in 2010. Workers are assumed to have the same relative level of earnings throughout their careers.
[b] OASDI contributions were based on SSA 1992 tax rate of 6.2% and maximum earnings of $55,000.
[c] WB = Workers benefit, SB = Spousal benefit.

Source: United States House Select Committee on Aging, *How Well Do Women Fare Under the Nation's Retirement Policies?* Hearing Before the Subcommittee on Retirement Income and Employment of the Select Committee on Aging, House of Representatives, One Hundred First Congress, second session. Washington, D.C.: U.S. Government Printing Office, September, 1992.

In 1992, 92% of women age 65 and older received Social Security (Older Women's League, 1995). Virtually all baby boom women will receive Social Security benefits. Today, it is widely assumed that baby boom women's labor force participation will ensure their eligibility for Social Security based on their own earnings record. At this time, it is difficult to forecast what the distribution by type of entitlement will be for baby boom women. If few or no changes occur in the Social Security system, the pattern displayed in Table 33 may continue for female boomers—minimal percentage changes in worker-only eligibility, increases in dual entitlement and decreases in spousal-only benefits.

Changes to the Social Security system that consider and/or factor in women's issues are highly unlikely for the foreseeable future. The fiscal and political climate in the United States has essentially curtailed any reforms relating to women's issues. Equity and adequacy issues continue to plague the Social Security system (e.g., equity for dual-earner couples, recognition of the economic value of child rearing and homemaking, and more equitable and adequate benefits for widows and divorced women) (Ross & Upp, 1993). Current proposed legislation to alter the Social Security system focuses on controlling the growth of entitlement spending, not on reforming the system of social insurance and transfers. Examples of proposals being discussed are:

- gradually raise the age of full eligibility for Social Security retirement benefits from 67 to 70 to reflect longer life spans;

- gradually raise the age of early eligibility from 62 to 65 by 2017;

- limit cost-of-living allowances (COLAs) for all beneficiaries to that received by beneficiaries in the 30th percentile of benefits;

- study the accuracy of the Consumer Price Index to determine the size of COLAs for Social Security and federal retirement;

- allow workers to divert 2% out of their 6.2% Social Security payroll tax to IRA-type accounts controlled by them, not the government;

- invest up to 25% of Social Security Trust Fund assets in equities, rather than Treasury securities (Cornman & Kingson, 1996; Wyatt, 1995).

These, and other, recommended changes to Social Security attempt to fine-tune the existing system. They in no way look to change the structure of Social Security which may be necessary to address women's issues. Additionally, policymakers have yet to really discuss the implications of baby boom retirement, let alone the needs of baby boom women (Feldstein, 1996; Schieber & Shoven, 1996).

Pension Income for Baby Boom Women

Since 1950, pension coverage has undergone two substantial changes. The first is a function of the changing nature of work; the second, a function of the changing nature of the employer-employee relationship.

These changes will transform the role of pensions in baby boomers' retirement.

Pension coverage among full-time wage and salary employees in the private sector more than doubled between 1950 and 1979 (Manchester, 1993). As the baby boom moved into the labor market, the growth in pension coverage slowed considerably and has essentially remained stable since 1975. About half of today's workers are covered by an employer-provided pension plan (U.S. Department of Labor, 1995b). Kingson (1992) attributes the lack of growth in pension coverage to the changing nature of work—the loss of manufacturing jobs and the increase of service sector jobs. The decline of unionized industries, where pension coverage is high, contributed significantly to this stagnation; 90% of union workers participate in a pension plan compared to 55% of their non-union counterparts (Wiatrowski, 1993).

Over the past twenty years, the mix of pension plans available to workers has changed, characterizing the shift in the employer-employee relationship. Defined benefit coverage has declined while defined contribution coverage is rising. The traditional pension, defined benefit, which continues to provide the majority of coverage, is rapidly being replaced by voluntary retirement savings plans, in particular, the 401(k) defined contribution plan (Woods, 1993). The fundamental differences between the two types of pension plans are:

- Defined benefit plans are designed to provide the highest replacement rate to workers who are covered by one plan throughout their work life. The emphasis of this type of plan is future pension payments. Defined benefit plans guarantee a specific benefit amount based on factors such as the employee's salary and years of service. Benefits are usually provided through a life annuity. These annuity-type benefits are generally financed and managed entirely by the employer (U.S. Department of Labor, 1995b).

- Defined contribution plans have features that are more beneficial to employees who work for several employees over their work life. The focus is on accumulating funds. Defined contribution plans do not guarantee a specific benefit amount. It bases benefits on the company's and/or worker's contributions and the interest earned on the plan's investments. Defined contribution plans permit retiring or terminated employees to receive a lump-sum distribution of the vested value of their account (U.S. Department of Labor, 1995b).

Table 35 illustrates the growth in defined contribution plans between 1988 and 1993. By 1993, 58% of men and 53% of women workers were covered under some form of employer-sponsored retirement plan.

Coverage in defined contribution plans increased, 8% in 1988 to 17% in 1993. Coverage rates for women increased 49% to 53% due entirely to the growth in 401(k)-only coverage (Woods, 1994).

Table 35
Type of Coverage Under Employer-Sponsored Retirement Plans on Current Primary Job, 1988 and 1993, by Sex: Wage and Salary Workers Aged 25–54

Type of Coverage	1988	1993
Total percent covered	54	55
401(k)-type coverage only[1]	8	17
Other plan(s)only	37	28
Both 401(k) and other plan(s)	9	10
Men, total percent covered	59	58
401(k)-type coverage only[1]	10	18
Other plan(s) only	39	27
Both 401(k) and other plan(s)	10	12
Women, total percent covered	49	53
401(k)-type coverage only[1]	8	16
Other plan(s) only	34	28
Both 401(k) and other plan(s)	8	9

[1] The term "401(k) plan" refers to several kinds of employer-sponsored retirement plans that allow participating employees to make tax-deferred contributions to the plan, usually with some matching contribution from the employer.
Source: Woods, John R., "Pension Coverage Among the Baby Boomers: Initial Findings from a 1993 Survey." *Social Security Bulletin*. 57, no. 3 (Fall, 1994).

The baby boom should profit from the expansion in pension coverage resulting from legislative mandates (Employee Retirement Income Security Act (ERISA) of 1974, Retirement Equity Act (REA) of 1984, the 1986 Tax Reform Act (TRA), and changes in vesting rules. Among retirees, aged 55 and older, 48% reported employer-provided pension benefits representing about 19% of their entire retirement income (U.S. Department of Labor, 1995b). In 1993, 58% of baby boom men and 52% of baby boom women were covered by an employer-sponsored retirement plan. "Early" boomers, male (64%) and female (56%) have slightly higher rates of coverage than "later" male (52%) and female (48%) boomers (Figure 17). By the time all baby boomers have reached retirement age in 2030, it is anticipated that pension coverage will expand to 82% of baby boomers (Table 30) representing 24% of their entire retirement income (Figure 15). These numbers, quite high compared to current pension coverage, assume that lump-sum distributions are rolled over each time a worker changes jobs, and income is paid out as an annuity (Salisbury, 1995). While their parents receive pension income primarily from one employer, baby boomers are likely to receive multiple pensions from the various employers throughout their labor force careers (AARP, 1994).

While this is good news for the cohort, there are two trends in pension coverage that do not bode well for baby boomers, especially female boomers. The first is the risk associated with defined contribution plans; there are no income guarantees. The second trend involves the distribution of future pension benefits. Many of the pensions baby boomers will receive will be modest with about one third of all boomers receiving only 5% or less of their income from pensions (AARP, 1994). Woods (1994) warns that a pattern between "early" and "later" boomers is appearing—primarily an increase in 401(k)-only coverage among the "later" boomers (Table 36). Concern about this pattern applies to baby boom women also, since they are more likely to participate in defined contribution plans than defined benefit plans.

Figure 17
Percent of Baby Boomers Covered by an Employer-Sponsored Retirement Plan, 1993

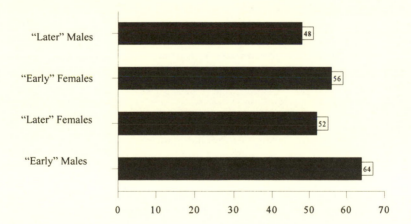

Source: Adapted from Woods, John R., "Pension Coverage Among the Baby Boomers: Initial Findings from a 1993 Survey." *Social Security Bulletin*. 57, no. 3 (Fall, 1994).

For the baby boom, the net effect of the growth of defined contribution plans has been a significant increase in pension coverage for women with a corresponding decline in "other" coverage, specifically defined benefit coverage, for men. Highly mobile workers and workers with interrupted work careers (i.e., baby boom women) benefit from this change since it offers improved pension portability. While the availability of retirement plans has expanded to include baby boom women, the overall risk to retirement savings has increased significantly for both baby boom men and women.

Table 36
Type of Coverage Under Employer-Sponsored Retirement Plans on Current Primary Job, by Sex, in April, 1993: Percentage Distribution of *Covered* "Early" and "Later" Baby Boom Wage and Salary Workers

Age of Worker	Type of Coverage (Percent)		
	401(k)-Type Plan Only[1]	Other Type of Plan(s) Only	Both 401(k)-Type Plan and Other Plan(s)
Men 37–46 (early boomers) 27–36 (later boomers)	29 37	48 45	23 19
Women 37–46 (early boomers) 27–36 (later boomers)	27 33	55 52	17 14

[1] The term "401(k) plan" refers to several kinds of employer-sponsored retirement plans that allow participating employees to make tax-deferred contributions to the plan, usually with some matching contribution from the employer.
Source: Woods, John R., "Pension Coverage Among the Baby Boomers: Initial Findings from a 1993 Survey." *Social Security Bulletin.* 57, no. 3 (Fall, 1994).

The inherent uncertainty in defined contribution plans (compared to defined benefit plans) is evidenced by the trends listed below. They all have significance for the future retirement security of the baby boom, especially for baby boom women.

• Shift from non-elective employer contributions to elective employee contributions. Disagreement abounds about what the contribution levels should be to yield adequate retirement benefits. Some analysts say total annual contribution, between employee and employer, should be about 10% of the employee's salary; others contend 5% of salary over a full career is sufficient. Among "early" and "later" boomers, male and female, who had only 401(k)s, average annual contributions were 6.7 and 6.3% of wages, respectively (Woods, 1994).

- Shift from plan-directed investment to participant-directed investment. Typically, 401(k) participants are offered a limited set of investment options. Employees are responsible for choosing how to invest and manage their money. Recent evidence shows that workers tend to make very conservative investment choices that yield lower and potentially inadequate returns (National Academy on Aging, 1994; Woods, 1994).

- Growing availability and pre-retirement "cash-out" of lump-sum distribution from pension plans. The portability of defined contribution plans permits employees to receive a lump sum at job termination that can be "rolled over" into an Individual Retirement Plan (IRA) or another employer's plan without tax penalty. The concern is asset preservation— will baby boomers save this money for their retirement or will they spend it? Recent data seems to indicate that as boomers age, there is a greater tendency to save rather than spend (U.S. Department of Labor, 1995b).

- There are no guarantees regarding accumulation of assets or a promised level of benefit since the onus of responsibility has shifted from employer to employee.

- Pension laws allow firms to exclude part-time workers from participating in tax-qualified plans (Even & Macpherson, 1994). Less than 20% of part-time workers participate in employer-sponsored pension plans (Rix, 1993).

The other continuing trend that will greatly impact retirement income for baby boomers is the distribution of pension income. Current projections indicate that by 2030, the average pension income will be $11,245, whereas the median income will be only $5,935 (AARP, 1994). These figures indicate that a small number of baby boomers will have high pension income and a large number will have small pensions. It is certain that the polarization of income will continue during the retirement years of the baby boom. Few baby boom women will be recipients of high pension income.

For baby boom women, there is yet another continuing trend that will negatively impact future pension income. A gender gap in pension coverage exists (Even & Macpherson, 1994). In 1994, 57% of male retirees aged 55 and over received pension benefits; only 38% of women retirees did. Men received median annual benefits of $9,600 and mean annual benefits of $14,654; women received median annual benefits of $4,800 and mean annual benefits of $6,748. Women's pension income in 1994 equaled 50% of men's benefits, up from 37% in 1989 (U.S.

Department of Labor, 1995b).   This gender gap is slowly narrowing but it will continue to exist for baby boom women.

The gender gap in coverage among the employed will eventually translate into a gender gap in the retired population. Baby boom women's labor force participation will narrow the gap in pension coverage, but it does not alter the fact that baby boom women work in industries and occupations least likely to have private pension plans (Calasanti, 1993). Additionally, the statistics about pension coverage track workers who are *eligible* for coverage under an employer-sponsored retirement plan. It does not measure participation. According to the U.S. Department of Labor, in 1993, 33% of all full-time women workers were eligible to contribute to a 401(k) plan, but only 20% did. The reason for this lack of participation is that lower-paid workers often cannot afford to participate (Borzi, 1995). Even and Macpherson (1994) suggest that the gender gap is a function of women's labor force participation patterns and that pension coverage is less likely to convert into pension receipt at retirement. While changes in vesting rules have actually helped baby boom women acquire pension coverage, women's job tenure and propensity for part-time work are major obstacles to accruing pension income. Women have shorter job tenure, on average, than men, reducing the likelihood that a woman will become fully vested and earn all rights to a pension benefit. Recent estimates show that average job tenure for a woman is 4.8 years (Karpel, 1995). Most employer-sponsored pension plans have vesting schedules of at least five years. In addition, it is common for employers to require that a new employee work a full year before she is eligible to participate in the company's retirement plan. Therefore, a woman who works for an employer for only 4.8 years will never vest in a retirement plan (Patterson, 1995).

Compounding the vesting paradox is the fact that nearly a third of baby boom women worked part-time in 1990 and the majority will work part-time at some point during their careers (see Chapter 4). As noted earlier, employers are not required to include part-time workers in their defined contribution plans. Another paradox seems to exist for baby boom women—while defined contribution plans opened the window to pension coverage for baby boom women, the window is closed to nearly one third of working female boomers.

What is the likelihood that a baby boom woman will receive pension income? Women who are most attached to the labor market are the most likely to locate a job with a pension (Even & Macpherson, 1994). Pension receipt is highly correlated to three variables: pre-retirement income levels (Figure 18), the size of the primary employer (Figure 19), and the educational attainment of the individual (Figure 20) (U.S. Department of Labor, 1995b; U.S. Department of Labor, 1994). Table 37 describes which female boomers will most/least likely receive a pension upon retirement.

Figure 18
Pension Benefit Receipt Rates for Retirees 55+ by Pre-Retirement Wage Levels

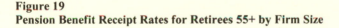
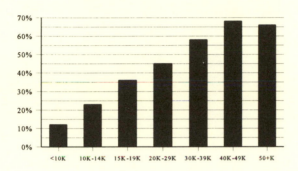

Source: U.S. Department of Labor, "Retirement Benefits of American Workers: New Findings from September, 1994." *Current Population Survey*. Washington, D.C.: 1995.

Figure 19
Pension Benefit Receipt Rates for Retirees 55+ by Firm Size

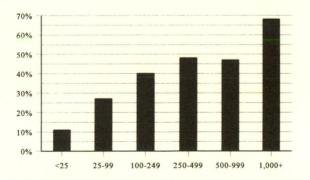
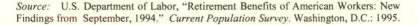

Source: U.S. Department of Labor, "Retirement Benefits of American Workers: New Findings from September, 1994." *Current Population Survey*. Washington, D.C.: 1995.

Figure 20
Pension Benefit Receipt Rates for Retirees 55+ by Education Level

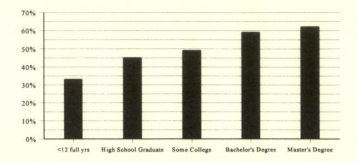

Source: U.S. Department of Labor, "Retirement Benefits of American Workers: New Findings from September, 1994." *Current Population Survey.* Washington, D.C.: 1995.

Table 37
Female Boomers Most/Least Likely to Receive a Pension

A female boomer most likely to receive a pension upon retirement will: • make $40,000+ per year • work for a large company (+1,000 employees) • possess a master's degree	A female boomer least likely to receive a pension upon retirement will: • make less than $10,000+ per year • work for a small company (<25 employees) • not have a high school diploma

A woman who works in a managerial or professional specialty will be most likely to receive a pension since higher earnings are generally associated with those occupations. Only 13.7% of baby boom women were employed in these occupations in 1990. Baby boom women with five years or more of college had a labor force participation rate of 86%; baby boom women with less than four years of high school had a participation rate of 53% (see Chapter 4). It is not known how many baby boom women work for large-sized companies, but it is known that most women are employed by small- and medium-sized firms who often do not offer retirement benefits. Nearly half of all employed women work for employers who do not provide pension plans to their employees (Rix, 1993). These conditions make forecasting of baby boom women's future pension income very imprecise.

Baby boom women will receive pension income at their retirement. At question is what percentage of baby boom women will actually receive pension income and how much can they expect to collect. Like labor force participation rates, pension coverage rates reveal very little about the financial future for baby boom women. Baby boom women have increased access to pension coverage, yet this does not necessarily translate into pension receipt. Obstacles to pension receipt include low wages, vesting schedules, part-time work, size of employer, and educational attainment. While 82% of the baby boom are expected to receive pension income (Table 30), baby boom women should not assume that they will collect on these benefits.

Asset Income for Baby Boom Women

Our society has long considered personal savings the "safety net" for income replacement during retirement (Wiatrowski, 1993). If Social Security and employer pension benefits are inadequate, personal savings or asset income is expected to make up the difference. As part of the life cycle, it is assumed that people will naturally accumulate savings, home equity, and personal property by the time they reach retirement age (U.S. House Select Committee on Aging, 1992). On this assumption, it is expected that 90% of baby boomers will have asset income (Table 30).

Assets are measured in terms of net worth and include such vehicles as home equity, Individual Retirement Accounts (IRAs), savings accounts, investments, real estate, business, even inheritances. The largest share of asset income for today's elderly is in the form of home equity, about 40% (Figure 21).

Asset income is projected to represent about 23% of the baby boom's retirement income (Figure 15), about the same as for their parents (21%). However, asset income, or personal savings, is the biggest unknown in the retirement income equation, especially for baby boom women. The variability in predicting baby boom savings rates, performance of investment vehicles, capital gains, future economic conditions, or windfalls from inheritances allows for only broad assumptions about the impact of asset income on baby boomers' retirement.

As with their elders, much of the baby boom wealth is in housing (National Academy on Aging, 1994). About two-thirds of baby boomers own their own homes. "Early" baby boomers have higher rates of home ownership (71%) than "later" boomers (57%). Single baby boomers are much less likely to be homeowners (46%) (AARP, 1994). Home ownership is considered a good indicator of the potential for life time earnings although the role it will play in financing the retirement of the baby boom is uncertain (Manchester, 1993). Baby boomers may not enjoy the same rates of return that home ownership has afforded their parents. Housing prices have barely kept up with inflation over the past ten years. Housing values are likely to rise no faster than inflation for the next decade, which may make home ownership less attractive as a savings vehicle for the baby boom (O'Reilly, 1995). Additionally, baby boomers may have reduced the value of their home as a vehicle for retirement savings given the increase in home equity loans in recent years (National Academy on Aging, 1994).

Figure 21
Distribution of Net Worth by Asset Type for Older Households, 1988

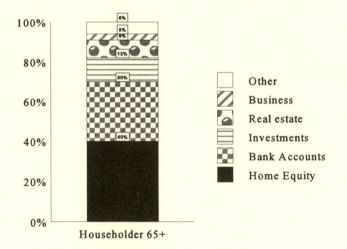

Source: United States Congress House Select Committee on Aging, "Aging in America: Trends and Projections." Washington, D.C.: U.S. Government Printing Office. 1991.

There is much debate about personal savings rates for the baby boom. On average, personal savings reach their highest level between the ages of 45 and 64, and are at their lowest level between ages 25–44, presumably because of the large expenses of child rearing and household formation (Cantor & Yuengert, 1994). The baby boom is just now moving into an age where they may be able to save more for their retirement. Some baby boomers will be more likely than others to increase personal savings. It is anticipated that while 90% of baby boomers will receive some form of asset income during retirement, those with higher incomes will get a disproportionate share. The chances of being able to increase personal savings for retirement is much greater for baby boomers who are white, non-Hispanic, married and living with their spouses, college educated, and/or born before 1955 (AARP, 1994).

Asset income is difficult to predict for baby boom women since many variables—marital status, education, children, home ownership, labor force participation, wage levels, pension coverage—will influence their ability to save over the next twenty years. If higher earnings, higher education, and current home ownership are good indicators of future asset income, only a limited number of baby boom women will accrue significant amounts of asset income. The majority of baby boom women will rely more heavily on Social Security and pension income for their sources of retirement. If these sources are inadequate, female boomers will need to turn to earnings income as their "safety net."

Earnings Income for Baby Boom Women

Another area of debate regarding the future of the baby boom is whether or not the trend toward early retirement will continue as boomers move closer to retirement age. Most of the projections for the baby boom assume that the baby boom will take early retirement and the labor force participation rates of the elderly will continue to decline (AARP, 1994; Manchester, 1993; Andrews & Chollet, 1988). These forecasts presume that people retire as soon as it is financially feasible. In fact, the majority of today's retired Americans cannot or do not want to work (Quinn & Burkhauser, 1994). By the year 2030, only 14% of baby boomers, primarily "later" boomers, are projected to be working past their normal retirement age. Only 6.5% of female boomers are expected to have earnings income when "early" female boomers have reached normal retirement age in 2010 (Table 38). When all baby boomers have reached normal retirement age, only 6% of female boomers are projected to be in the paid labor market.

Earnings as a source of retirement income appears to be rather insignificant for baby boom women. The most important predictors of employment past retirement age for women are (1) being single; and (2) not receiving any other pension in addition to Social Security (Rayman,

Allshouse & Allen, 1993). By 2030, 4.2% of female boomers, twice as many as baby boom men, will fall into this category (Table 31). These women will be forced to choose between one of two options: retirement on inadequate or barely adequate benefits or putting off retirement. Women who will need to work will face obstacles in finding employment due to limited job skills, age and sex discrimination, and caregiving responsibilities (Rix, 1993). Conventional wisdom suggests that women with the economic need for employment during old age will have the most difficulty locating and/or keeping jobs. Baby boom women most likely to be poor and in need of earnings income will be divorced, single or widowed. There will be more divorced baby boom women at retirement compared to today's elderly women. The mothers of baby boom women are more likely to be widows than divorcées. This is of significance for female boomers since a widow receives 100% of her spouse's worker benefit but a divorcée receives only 50% for as long as her ex-husband is alive (Rayman, Allshouse & Allen, 1993).

Table 38
Labor Force Participation Rates of Persons Age 65 and Over, 1950–2030, Actual and Projected

Year	Men	Women
1950	45.8%	9.7%
1960	33.1	10.8
1970	26.8	9.7
1980	19.1	8.1
1990	16.4	8.7
2000	12.9	6.9
2010	11.7	6.2
2020	11.7	6.5
2030	10.9	6.0

Source: American Association of Retired Persons, *Aging Baby Boomers: How Secure Is Their Economic Future?* Washington, D.C.: 1994. Booklet.

Current forecasts suggest that very few baby boom women will be in the paid labor market as they age, given that the majority (70%) of women will have access to the three most important sources of retirement income—Social Security, pension, and asset income. What these projections may be masking is that while female boomers will be working, they just won't receive earnings. Their dual roles as wage earner and home maker will most likely convert to caregiver for an elderly parent, spouse or sibling. What is unknown is whether baby boom women will leave paid labor because they are financially able or because it is financially expedient for the family due to the expense of elder care.

Families will provide over 80% of long-term care for the frail elderly by the year 2030 (Addleman, 1995). This statement is somewhat misleading in that it should read "women" will provide long-term care. Studies show that daughters are consistently more likely than sons to provide higher levels of personal care, "hands-on," daily assistance. Sons are more likely to provide periodic help such as home repair and financial management (Kramer & Kipnis, 1995; Mui, 1995). About three-quarters of all informal caregivers of the elderly are women: 29% are daughters, 23% are wives, and 20% are other females such as daughters-in-law; the figures for sons, husbands and other males are 8%, 13% and 7% (Ettner, 1995).

Forecasts of the baby boom's retirement rarely discuss the impact caregiving will have on women's retirement decisions or their financial security in retirement. At the front end of a baby boom woman's labor force participation years, she will lose time (either in unpaid leave or in part-time, part-year status) from work to care for children. Toward the close of her career as wage earner, she will very likely lose time to care for an elderly relative. Both instances will ultimately reduce her Social Security and pension incomes. A 1989 Employee Benefits Research Institute study found that 31% of those surveyed who provided elder care had refused a promotion, reduced working hours, retired early, or stopped working to fulfill their caregiving responsibilities (EBRI, 1993).

There is little question that baby boom women will be given the caregiving burden of our aging society. What is at question is whether they will be less tolerant of this burden than prior generations of women. Employment did not decrease women's care giving responsibilities for children. Employment will not decrease the likelihood of becoming a caregiver for an elderly relative (Barnes, Given & Given, 1995; Robison, Moen & Dempster-McClain, 1995). Baby boom women, unlike their male counterparts, will be forced to make difficult trade-offs between labor, leisure, and caregiving time as they approach retirement. These decisions, coupled with the decisions made in early adulthood regarding education, marriage, children, and labor force participation, will determine their retirement experience.

SUMMARY

At this point in time, the prognosis of a secure retirement for the baby boom looks good despite the "doomsayers." The "bright" outlook for baby boom women could be a reality but not without intervention by women today to take control of their financial future. Baby boom women need to question several primary outcomes about their future retirement income that are implied in projections about the baby boom's retirement. The in-depth review of retirement income sources conducted in this chapter now makes it possible to extract the general assumptions that are commonly held regarding the future of women's retirement. These assumptions need to be challenged by baby boom women:

- Assumption #1: *Baby boom women will be the first generation of women who will have earned their own retirement as a worker, not as a spouse.* For some women this will be true but many will be disappointed to learn that their Social Security spousal benefit will be higher than their worker's benefit. Even though they have worked all their adult lives, many will not have "earned" the right to retire on their own.

- Assumption #2: *Baby boom women's labor force participation will make them eligible for their own pensions.* Pension coverage is not pension receipt. The nature of work for baby boom women could very well diminish opportunities for actual pension receipt. If women do receive pension benefits it will most likely be a small, one-time, lump-sum distribution.

- Assumption #3: *Asset income, the third leg of the income "stool," will be an important part of retirement income; 90% of baby boomers can expect to receive some form of asset income.* Asset income will either be minimal or non-existent for the majority of baby boom women. Baby boom women will have great difficultly accruing personal savings. Home ownership is even at risk given the divorce rates of baby boom marriages.

- Assumption #4: *Baby boom women will not work in old age.* They may not get paid but they certainly will be working as caregivers to the elderly.

The message for baby boom women is clear: baby boom women need to prepare and plan for retirement primarily because they are at a financial disadvantage. They earn less than men, have less access to defined benefit coverage, have more difficulty saving, and carry the caregiving burden for children and the elderly. These differences point to a more precarious financial future for women than for men. It is further aggravated by the fact that baby boom women are expected to outlive their spouses by fifteen years (see Chapter 3). Therefore, what, if anything are baby boom women currently doing to prepare and plan for their retirement years? Very little research has been done to answer this question; what has been done indicates that very few women prepare for retirement—especially regarding financial planning (Hayes & Parker, 1993). The best educated generation ever is functionally illiterate when it comes to personal finances (Krysty, 1995). This is even more true for baby boom women. Feuerbach and Erdwins (1994) state that women, in general, tend not to think about retirement. Their retirement knowledge is extremely limited. Perkins (1992) offers a psychosocial explanation: "Because of the prevailing 'myth' among women that they will be cared for in old age and women's fear of growing old, women often do not aggressively plan for their retirement." Others argue that many women approach retirement age without the financial resources (due to a life time of inferior earnings) necessary for meaningful planning (Kilty & Behling, 1986).

At this point in time, baby boom women, even the most committed women workers, will need to rely on the resources of their spouses during retirement. Logue (1991) sums up the precariousness of many women's economic situation: "They may be one husband away from poverty." Regardless of the obstacles, financial or psychosocial, if baby boom women want some control over their financial future, they will need to be actively engaged in the planning and preparation of their retirement years. Baby boom women cannot afford to be passive participants in the retirement process. They need to learn more about money management, overcome their risk aversion to investments and understand that the decisions they make regarding education, marriage, children, type of occupation, type of employer (small/large firms), etc., will culminate in a retirement income that will sustain their old age or push them into poverty. The system of elder income within our retirement structure is deeply anchored in our society and is expected to sustain baby boom women's retirement. However, for many baby boom women, this system produces multiple risks that may threaten their retirement future. In-depth analysis of baby boom women's financial outlook confirms the fact that "appearances" can mask the true nature of a structure.

6

Baby Boom Women's Retirement Future

The American economy has shifted from agriculture to industry to services in a very short period of time, in less than two hundred years. One of the structural by-products of this economic transformation is the institution of retirement; an institution firmly entrenched in our society. The notion of an "earned" right to freedom from a forty-hour work week, from the same routine, from supervision, has penetrated the American worker psyche (Calasanti, 1993). Baby boom men and women look to their old age with this vision of retirement, this freedom from labor, as their reward for years of hard work. Baby boomers are now witnessing this vision when they view their parents' retirement years.

As the economy continues to shift and as the nature of work changes, so must the vision of retirement. This study concludes that the vision of retirement for the baby boom generation is unclear, especially for baby boom women. Debate about the retirement future of the baby boom continues and becomes more passionate as the baby boom ages, often obscuring issues vital to women's economic prospects. Many question if the American dream is at risk while others see a brighter future; some advise drastic interventions, others caution gradual adaptation. In spite of this debate, the history of institutionalization brings with it an inertia that continues to support current retirement practices (Birren, et al., 1986). The institutional mechanisms (i.e., Social Security, pensions, Medicare, etc.) that currently run the retirement machine are expected to also provide for the baby boom. The efficacy of retirement as a social institution for the baby boom generation has never been in doubt. What is being questioned is the future level and adequacy of their retirement living. Data analysis in this study has made it quite obvious that financial security in retirement is of critical importance to baby boom women.

Baby boom women will be the first generation of women to have the option of defining their own retirement. They are the first female cohort whose labor force participation will span most of their adult life. However, their work life experience is not a mirror image of their male counterparts'. As this study revealed, even if women have comparable levels of education or income, their social and family role commitments impact their labor force participation, which will, ultimately, make their retirement experience different from that of men.

Until recently, women's retirement was considered a subset of men's retirement, an ancillary event that complemented male retirement. Retirement was portrayed as inconsequential for women or their families. Any effect was considered positive since retirement enabled women to disengage from the stresses of maintaining dual roles (wage earner and homemaker) to return full-time to their primary social role of care-giving (Hatch & Thompson, 1990). The assumption of retirement's unimportance to women's lives, especially married women, continued until the 1980s (Slevin and Wingrove, 1995; Wise, 1990; Gratton and Haug, 1983). Vestiges of this perspective still linger, given the minimal amount of study and data about women's retirement that has been generated over the past decade.

The massive entry of baby boom women into the labor force now makes retirement important for working women. It comes at a time when existing research models and data are outdated and inadequate to effectively predict their future retirement experience. This study shows that continued use of the linear, undifferentiated model of traditional male retirement will mislead, confuse and compound this research dilemma. Researchers need to be ever watchful of the historical biases toward women's retirement. A research model that accurately reflects the predictors and parameters of baby boom women's retirement, such as those identified in this book, will consider the social and work structures that influence women's lives.

Baby boom women's life choices are considerably more complex and diverse than those of previous female cohorts. As the center of analysis, baby boom women's future retirement can best be understood from a life-course perspective. The traditional and popular notion of retirement as a single, isolated event that ends a person's labor force participation is woefully inadequate to describe retirement for baby boom women. An accumulation of advantages and disadvantages will display itself in the form of highly varied retirement experiences for baby boom women (Hayward & Grady, 1990). For baby boom men and women, retirement will be a complex process that accounts for individual work life circumstances as well as important life events.

The implicit assumptions introduced in Chapter 1 regarding baby boom women and baby boom retirement have been challenged throughout this book. The first two assumptions have been debunked while the third has been confirmed:

- Assumption #1: Women's retirement will resemble men's retirement since their labor force patterns look similar.

- Assumption #2: The traditional three-legged stool of retirement income—Social Security, employer pensions and personal savings—will continue to finance baby boom retirement. The retirement blueprint used for their parents will suffice for the baby boom.

- Assumption #3: Women will continue as society's caregivers regardless of their labor force participation. The difference for baby boom women will be the extension of this care from children to the elderly.

The following summary outlines the results of this study.

SUMMARY FINDINGS

A gestalt approach to the research questions was utilized to address the complexity of this macro level inquiry. Study of baby boom women's retirement required a multivariate analysis that incorporated observation of the nature of work and retirement for women in our society. Answers to the research questions are woven and integrated throughout the content chapters. The following summary answers, directly and indirectly, the research questions used to formulate this study.

Study of the three macro level variables—population aging, labor force participation, and retirement income sources—scrutinized the structural properties of baby boom women's labor force attachment and recognized the impact demographic shifts have had or will have on baby boom women's life choices. These structural variables were selected for inquiry because they clearly revealed the gendered nature of work and retirement and the dialectical relations between work and family for women.

Population Aging

As a cohort group, baby boom women have had and will continue to have a profound influence on the aging of the United States population.

Baby boom women's life choices strongly impact two of the three factors used to determine age structure—fertility and mortality. Conversely, these two variables will definitively shape baby boom women's retirement destiny.

Evidence that the population of the United States is aging can be seen in: (1) the significant rise in the 65 and over population; (2) the sharp rise in median age; (3) the larger fraction of the "old-old" or those over the age of 85; (4) falling birth rates; and (5) the decline in the proportion of children in the population. American society is experiencing what demographers call the "double aging" process—shrinking numbers of younger persons occurring simultaneously with expansion of the elderly population (Borsch-Supan, 1992). "Double aging" will have profound effect on baby boom women's retirement because of their role in childbearing and caregiving.

Fertility is the most unpredictable variable in the population aging equation since it involves individual choice. Decisions can be swayed by many social and economic factors as well as by social class and ethnic and generation characteristics (Preston, 1993). A woman's decision about childbearing has broad, social repercussions as well as personal consequences. The life choices made by baby boom women have produced a fertility rate that guarantees the aging of the population. Most all baby boom women will be mothers; it is estimated about 85% will bear children. They will have an average of close to two children.

Besides replacement ratios, the fertility behavior of baby boom women has had two significant side effects that will ultimately determine their retirement experience:

• For the mothers and grandmothers of baby boom women, childbearing and marriage were synonymous; for baby boom women they are not. Baby boom women have opted to have children despite the high level of marital instability in the United States. The decision to bear children, knowing that they face work-family conflicts or that they may be the sole supporter of their children, is an emerging demographic pattern. In 1990, approximately 14 million baby boom women (about one third) were single female heads of households.

• For the mothers and grandmothers of baby boom women, marriage was the key structural variable to predict their retirement experience. Changes in social mores concerning divorce, bearing children out of wedlock, singlehood, and women working outside the home have minimized marriage as a key structural variable for predicting baby boom women's retirement. Dependency on a spouse's retirement income will be a risky proposition for baby boom women. Marriage will continue to be a variable in predicting women's retirement but it will not hold the financial and social significance it did for their mothers. Marriage will be an advantage, not the sole indicator.

Motherhood and marriage have taken on distinctly different meanings for baby boom women. Baby boom women have chosen to have children later in life, to have fewer children and, for some, to bear children without being married first. They have had options regarding marriage and childbearing that were not available to their mothers' generation. Many baby boom women view these options as liberating, offering them life choices not known to their mothers. Whether baby boom women in old age see these changes in motherhood and marriage as liberating is yet to be determined. The changes in these social institutions may, in many ways, backfire on baby boom women. First, the mothers of baby boomers were, for the most part, guaranteed a secure retirement if they remained married. Baby boom women have no guarantees regarding marriage, let alone a secure retirement. Second, women's primary social role has in no way been altered. Rather, these changes to marriage and motherhood have served to cement women's role as society's caregivers. This will become very evident as the population continues to age.

Decline in mortality is the other demographic shift that is driving population aging. The most significant demographic change is the stunning growth of the old-old (85+) age group, most of whom are women. It is very likely that a baby boom woman will either become "old-old," care for an "old-old" relative, or both. Increases in life expectancy has produced two fundamental facts for baby boom women:

- Like their mothers, baby boom women can expect to be alone in their old age. If a baby boom woman reaches age 65, she can expect to live until age 85. For the majority of that time, she will be alone. She will likely be widowed at the age of 67 and remain a widow for fifteen years.

- Baby boom women will be the primary care providers of the country's frail elderly. The net effect of lower fertility and mortality declines is increased dependency. Baby boom women can anticipate caring for a parent, spouse, or sibling prior to and throughout their retirement years before becoming frail themselves.

Baby boom women will feel the burden of old-age dependency as they did the strains of child care and work. Many baby boom women will leave the work force or work part-time just when they will need to work for retirement benefits for their own old age or while they are adjusting to their own retirement, widowhood, and reduced incomes. This demographic forecast is a double-edge sword for a baby boom woman. While she may look forward to living to a ripe old age, her retirement years will most likely not be the "freedom from work" scenario that her mother experiences. Baby boom women will not be prepared, at least financially, for the social role expected of them regarding the primary care of the country's elderly.

Labor Force Participation

Women's labor force participation is the key driver of their future retirement experience. Understanding the nature of work for baby boom women validates or refutes many currently held assumptions and beliefs about women's work and their future retirement. A step-by-step examination by age, race, education, marital status, presence of children, work status (full-time/part-time; hours of work), and occupation exposed the true nature of work for baby boom women. These data paint a more accurate picture of work life for baby boom women and allow for more reliable projections of the future.

Baby boom women have changed female employment more than any other cohort group. A baby boom woman can expect to spend at least thirty years of her adult life in the paid labor force. In 1990, baby boom women ranged in age from 26–44, their peak productive work years. Three-quarters of them were in the labor market. White, married female boomers have been the force for change. These baby boom women rejected the conventional pattern of female employment and did not leave the paid labor force upon marriage or to care for children.

By 1990, work outside the home was the norm for women. Baby boom women's labor force participation by age now approximates the male model of employment, and any distinction between male and female median ages has disappeared. Unfortunately, a cursory look at these trends has promoted a popular misconception that women's employment simulates men's. This is partially true—but only as it relates to the participation rate by age. The more accurate interpretation of these data is that paid work has become a central part of women's lives even during their childbearing years.

The nature of work defines the social relations of baby boom women. As their demographic characteristics illustrate, women's labor force behavior does not resemble baby boom men's, aside from age. Baby boom women have redefined what female labor force participation means but have done so while making accommodations for their social role of caregiving. This is evidenced by:

- three out of four baby boom women work outside the home (Table 39); white baby boom women who are married with children reversed the traditional labor force participation pattern of their mothers.

- baby boom women have heavily invested in their human capital—almost 9 of

10 baby boom women are high school graduates and nearly one fourth are college educated (Table 40); baby boom women who are better educated will work longer, have shorter retirements and will have the most financial resources to draw from in retirement.

• children have a negative impact on women's employment, divorce has a positive impact on women's employment.

• full-time, year-round work is not the norm for all baby boom working women; the need for flexible schedules has lead baby boom working mothers, like their mothers before them, to part-time and/or part year work.

• presence of children and educational attainment will determine baby boom women's life time earnings potential.

Table 39
Female Labor Force Participation Rates by Birth Cohort

Year	Participation Rate					
	Age 16–19	Age 20–24	Age 25–34	Age 35–44	Age 45–54	Age 55–64
1960	39.1	46.1	35.8	43.1	49.3	36.7
1970	43.7	57.5	44.8	50.9	54.0	42.5
1980	52.9	68.9	65.5	65.5	59.9	41.3
1990	51.8	71.6	**73.6**	**76.5**	71.2	45.3

Sources: *1994 Statistical Abstract, 1980 Statistical Abstract.* United States Department of Commerce. Washington, D.C.

Table 40
Educational Attainment of Baby Boom Men and Women, 1990

Characteristic	Percent			
	Less Than High School	High School Graduate	Some College	College Graduate
All Baby Boomers	13.0	39.3	21.9	25.7
MEN Total	13.5	37.9	21.2	27.4
WOMEN Total	12.6	40.7	22.7	24.0

Source: U.S. Department of Labor, Bureau of Labor Statistics, unpublished tabulations from the *Current Population Survey,* 1990 annual averages.

Baby boom women have developed strong ties to the labor market that tolerate the pressures of marriage and child care. They have helped make it culturally acceptable for mothers to be breadwinners as well as caregivers, albeit, with some cost to their own personal economic future. Baby boom women have dramatically changed the composition of the labor force. On their road to permanent employment, they have created an age and race convergence, the dual-earner married couple, working mothers, and career women and mothers. They have made female labor force participation more diverse and less predictable. However, one variable that has remained unchanged is the role children play in defining women's paid employment. Baby boom women's labor force participation is shaped by motherhood. They are the primary care-takers of children and their labor force participation reflects this responsibility. It is this responsibility that allows gender differences to persist. Gender differences:

- in work experience (status) are a function of child care.

- in presence of children are negative for baby boom women, yet positive for men.

- in the occupational structure continue to reveal the duality of the labor market.

- in earnings will translate into a gender gap in retirement income.

Retirement Income for Women

Baby boom women will be the first generation of women to reap the benefits of retirement as workers, not as spouses. While this may be an historic first for women, it does not necessarily bode well for baby boom women. Retirement stands on the notion of "earned benefits" and it is clear that baby boom women will not "earn" the same right to retirement as their male counterparts. The social-contextual differences in baby boom women's work-life experiences will produce gendered retirement futures.

Financial security in retirement hinges on the assumption that baby boomers will have three sources (often referred to as the three-legged stool) from which to draw retirement income—Social Security, assets and pensions. Current projections indicate that Social Security will provide the largest share of income, followed by pension income and asset income. Earnings income is anticipated to play a relatively insignificant role in baby boom retirement income. Nearly all baby boomers will have Social Security income (98%), nine out of ten will receive some form of asset income, and the majority (82%) will have pension receipts.

A "bright future" is painted for those boomers with all three sources of retirement income. Projections indicate that nearly three-quarters of boomers will have access to all three sources. Of all baby boomers, those who are married and college-educated with high incomes will be the group most likely to have access to all three retirement sources; those least likely will be single females with a high school education or less who are poor or near-poor.

Analysis of income data and projections seems to bear out that baby boomers, on average, will be financially prepared for retirement. The "appearance" of current projections also concludes that the financial future of baby boom women looks promising. The assumptions of the "bright future" scenario need to be questioned, particularly the "on average" preface stipulated in the economic projections. Labor market inequities do not translate into "on average" income projections for women. Baby boom women will face a different financial future than their male counterparts because they:

- will have fewer years in the labor force.

- experience more interrupted work histories.

- are more concentrated in low-wage occupations.

- are less likely to work in industries with pension coverage.

- will receive lower Social Security benefits.

- will accumulate less in the way of assets and savings.

As with labor force participation rates, a closer look at retirement income for women is warranted to validate or refute predictions about the financial future for baby boom women.

Baby boom women will qualify for Social Security benefits in one of three ways—worker benefits, spousal benefits or dual entitlement benefits. Whether the majority of baby boom women qualify for worker benefits is in some doubt. Their life-long earnings gap will intersect with the provisions of Social Security, specifically zero averaging, to produce lower "worker" benefits. It appears that only one third of baby boom women will earn the right to maximize their Social Security earnings.

Spousal benefits will be available for those few baby boom women who do not accumulate the requisite number of quarters of coverage required for worker benefits. Few baby boom women will be eligible for entitlement solely as wives or widows. More important is female boomers' eligibility for dual entitlement. Dual entitlement is essentially a woman's benefit and will continue to be so for the baby boom generation. Dual entitlement benefits are necessary when a woman's life time earnings generate a Social Security benefit less than her benefit as a wife or widow.

The percentage of women receiving Social Security benefits based on their own work records has remained quite constant since 1960, in spite of women's increased labor force participation. In 1960, about 39% of women received "worker" benefits; by 1993, the proportion had changed little and had actually slightly decreased to 36%. The number of women who are dually entitled, on the other hand, has grown significantly, from 4.5% in 1960 to 25% in 1993. These trends in Social Security entitlement most likely will continue for baby boom women.

At this point in time, the exact number of baby boom women who will be dually entitled is unknown. Given the historical patterns of dual entitlement and the projection that only one third of baby boom women will maximize their Social Security earnings potential, it is very likely that a vast majority of baby boom women will receive dual entitlement benefits. The reality for married and divorced baby boom women is that many will retire as dually entitled. In terms of retirement income, it may have been better for many of these women not to have worked. The irony of the dual entitlement provision is that while working women pay payroll taxes for many years (reducing their ability to build personal savings) they do so for no additional benefits. It is highly likely that a woman with years of paid work experience would be entitled to higher Social Security benefits as the spouse of a retired worker than as a retired worker herself. A married woman who earns income and contributes to the system may not receive benefits any greater than if she had chosen not to work. Furthermore, because the Social Security system was created on the life-long breadwinner (male) model, a two-earner couple making the same income as a one-earner couple can end up paying thousands of dollars more in taxes for no increase in benefits. This will be very disappointing for many baby boom women who believe they have "earned" the right to retire on their own merits.

Pension receipt is expected to be another important source of baby boom retirement income. By the time all baby boomers have reached retirement age in 2030, it is anticipated that pension coverage will expand to 82% of baby boomers, representing 24% of their entire retirement income. This forecast, however, comes with several forewarnings. First, pension receipt is highly correlated to three variables: high pre-retirement earnings, employment by a large firm, and high educational attainment. Few baby boom women can boast all three variables. Second, income polarity will continue during the retirement years of the baby boom. Only a small number of baby boomers will have high pension income and a large number will have small pensions. Few baby boom women will be recipients of high pension income. Third, there are no income guarantees with defined contribution plans. This should be of concern to baby boom women since they are more likely to participate in defined contribution plans than defined benefit plans. Women will need to be financially self-reliant if they expect pension income to play a significant role in their retirement.

There are yet other caveats for baby boom women. Statistics about pension coverage track workers who are *eligible* for coverage under an employer-sponsored retirement plan. It does not measure participation. According to the U.S. Department of Labor, in 1993, 33% of all full-time women workers were eligible to contribute to a 401(k) plan, but only 20% did. The reason for this lack of participation is that lower-paid workers often cannot afford to participate (Borzi, 1995). Women's labor force participation patterns make it less likely that pension coverage will convert into pension receipt at retirement. While changes in vesting rules have actually helped baby boom women acquire pension coverage, women's job tenure and propensity for part-time work are major obstacles to accruing pension income.

Unknown for female boomers is the number of women who will actually receive pension income and how much they can expect to collect. The "appearance" of pension coverage rates seems to indicate that baby boom women will enjoy pension income upon retirement. However, like labor force participation rates, pension coverage rates reveal very little about the financial future for baby boom women. Baby boom women's labor force participation has increased their access to pension coverage, yet this does not guarantee pension receipt. While 82% of the baby boom is expected to receive pension income, baby boom women should not assume that they will collect on these benefits.

The third primary source of retirement income, asset income or personal savings, is projected to represent almost one quarter (23%) of the baby boom's retirement income. About 90% of baby boomers will receive some form of asset income during retirement. However, asset income projections, like those for pension income, come with a warning label. Baby boomers who have higher earnings, higher education and current home ownership will get a disproportionate share of asset income. Once again, few baby boom women have all three variables.

Personal savings is the biggest unknown in the retirement income equation. Asset income is difficult to predict for baby boom women since many variables—marital status, education, children, home ownership, labor force participation, wage levels, pension coverage—will influence their ability to save over the next twenty years. The majority of baby boom women will rely more heavily on Social Security and pension income in retirement. If these sources are inadequate, female boomers will need to turn to earnings income.

Current forecasts assume that the majority (70%) of baby boom women will have access to all three sources of retirement income, making it unnecessary for baby boom women in old age to be in the paid labor market. This prediction is somewhat disconcerting in light of the above discussions about baby boom women's access to retirement income sources. It is more likely that current projections about earnings income reflect society's tacit agreement that female boomers, in old age, will return to their primary social role of caregiver, not to children but to the country's frail elderly. Baby boom women will be working in their old age, they just won't receive earnings. What is unknown is whether baby boom women will leave paid labor because they are financially able or because it is financially expedient for the family due to the expense of elder care.

Baby boom women are at a financial disadvantage as they approach retirement. They earn less than men, have less access to pension coverage, have more difficulty saving, carry the caregiving burden for children and the elderly, and they can expect to outlive their spouses by fifteen years. The saving grace for baby boom women is that they still have time to prepare and plan for their financial futures.

CONCLUSION

Only a small number of baby boom women, less than 20%, should feel comfortable about their retirement future. Which baby boom women will do well in retirement? Women who are married, have a high education, women whose work lives look most like men's (uninterrupted work histories), women with high earnings, and women who own a home. Fewer than one fifth of baby boom women can meet these criteria and risk factors such as divorce, downsizing or disability will reduce their prospects. Marriage, education, occupation and home ownership—these are the variables that best predict the future for baby boom women. Baby boom women's retirement future can be viewed as a continuum with these variables stretched along its axis. Possession of all four variables indicates high retirement security; absence of any one of these variables increases risk of poverty in old age.

Since children are depicted to be the bane of baby boom women's labor force experience, how will they influence these women's retirement? In the context of their life cycle, the negative influence of children on labor force participation may reverse itself as baby boom women grow old. Some demographers and sociologists forecast that children will be the best insurance policy for baby boomers—for economic, social, and health care reasons. Having children may prove beneficial for female boomers in retirement. Society's care providers of the young and old will become the recipients of care themselves and those with children will be better off.

There is no one retirement future for baby boom women. Their demographics and life choices will determine their retirement destiny. However, the illusion of "being taken care of " in old age, a remnant of the traditional social structure, persists and must be shattered if baby boom women want a secure retirement. Women's retirement continues to be ignored. It is now time for baby boom women to think about their old age. Baby boom women cannot afford to be passive participants in the creation of their retirement destiny.

Of the three implicit assumptions held about baby boom women and baby boom retirement outlined earlier in this chapter, only one will likely prove true. Marital instability, single parenting, and new family structures have served to cement the caregiving role of women in our society. Employment in the paid labor market in no way diminishes this role. Baby boom women will shift their caregiving from children to the frail elderly as they move towards old age. This may be the biggest surprise of all for baby boom women. The vision of "freedom from work," for unstructured free time, for leisure, will materialize only for those with the financial means to avoid caregiving.

The expectation that the existing blueprint for retirement will suffice for baby boomers should send warning signals to women. Assumptions and implications about women's labor force participation and sources of retirement income need to be strongly challenged. The disparity between men and women's labor force experience guarantees differences in their financial future. Baby boom women's labor force participation arguably looks more like men's; however, when the true nature of women's work is revealed, a different picture emerges. Additionally, economic restructuring has upset the balance between government (Social Security), employer (pension income), and individual (asset income or personal savings) for the primary sources of retirement income. The traditional bond has weakened as employers redefine the rules of employment. This instability comes at a time when baby boom women have finally gained access to pension coverage.

"Two steps forward and one step back." This describes the social and economic progress baby boom women have made. Women have made great strides in their search for equality but not without placing themselves in economic jeopardy during their old age. Women's retirement will remain a subset of men's retirement. Like their mothers, baby boom women will need their spouses' retirement income to maintain their standard of living. The fundamental difference between the mothers of the baby boom and their daughters will be in the nature of the retirement experience. Baby boom women have shifted the relationship from one of dependency to one of interdependency. The husband of a baby boom woman may be just as likely to need her retirement income as she is to need his retirement income. In fact, the data revealed in this study should raise as many red flags about baby boom men's future as they do about women's retirement future.

Female boomers have done much to advance the social status of women yet their progress is steeped in irony:

• Baby boom women are redefining the institution of marriage yet marriage, as with their mothers, is their best bet for a secure retirement.

• Life-long employment for women is no guarantee of an "earned" entitlement to retirement.

• Working outside the home, even with young children, may not give a baby boom woman any more financial advantages in retirement. For many women, not working at all could prove more profitable in their old age.

• Just as women become eligible, pension benefits will most likely be minimal for the majority of baby boom women.

• Investment in human capital and increased labor force attachment offered self-sufficiency and some financial independence, but affirmed baby boom women's social role as caregiver.

If they do not take charge of their future now, baby boom women will be in for many unpleasant surprises as they approach their retirement years. Baby boom women need to be informed about what they can realistically expect in their old age and they need to act on their own behalf to secure their retirement. Women need to continue to invest in their education. They need to build job skills. They need to financially plan for their future and learn to manage their money and investments.

They need to seek jobs that offer pension plans. Finally, as difficult as it may be for many women to believe, the best insurance policy for baby boom women is to stay married. Marriage is an economic institution imbedded in our social structure. Female boomers have improved their social status, but one generation will not radically change the social structure, the nature of work or the nature of retirement for women.

POLICY IMPLICATIONS

At the policy level, what changes can baby boom women realistically expect, given the institutional inertia surrounding many of the structural elements impacting their economic and social future? Women will continue as society's caregivers; it is highly unlikely that current Social Security reform efforts will include discussion of women's needs; corporate America continues to push responsibility for retirement planning to the individual employee; and little discourse about the future of retirement for baby boomers is occurring. The best that baby boom women can expect at this juncture is to raise awareness about baby boom retirement and to raise the level of public discussion. Cornman and Kingson (1996) strongly urge mainstream policymakers to engage in a national conversation on the aging needs of our population rather than digress into a narrow debate about entitlement programs. A broad-based discourse about our shift to an aging society and the retirement of the baby boom may increase awareness that aging is very much a woman's issue, opening the door for an honest discussion about women's retirement needs.

The agenda for many organizations that promote and advise on women's policy issues (e.g., Older Women's League, Pension Rights Center, AARP's Women's Initiative group, the Center for Women's Policy Studies, etc.) has focused on pay equity, women's healthcare, age and sex discrimination, and women's poverty. These groups are currently lobbying against the proposal for Social Security privatization, to maintain Medicare solvency, and to address pension equity issues. Specific dialogue about baby boom women's future retirement has yet to get a place on their policy agendas. Baby boom women have a vested interest to see that it becomes an agenda item in the very near future while they have time to make changes, both on a personal level and a policy level, to create a secure retirement.

Bibliography

Addleman, Robert B. "Muppies and Eldercare." *Healthcare Forum Journal.* (May/June, 1995).

Althusser, Louis. *Politics and History: Montesquieu, Rousseau, Hegel and Marx.* London: New Left Books, 1977.

American Association of Retired Persons. *Aging Baby Boomers: How Secure is Their Economic Future?* Washington, D.C.: Author, 1994. Booklet.

_____. *Women, Pensions & Divorce.* Washington, D.C.: Author, 1993. Booklet.

_____. *America's Changing Work Force: Statistics in Brief.* Washington, D.C.: Author, 1988. Booklet.

American Association of Retired Persons and Administration on Aging. *A Profile of Older Americans.* Washington, D.C.: Author, 1995. Pamphlet.

_____. *A Profile of Older Americans.* Washington, D.C.: Author, 1993. Pamphlet.

American Demographics. "A Slow Fade for the Echo Boom." 16, no. 7 (July 1994):15–16.

_____. "Career Hopping." 15, no. 12 (December, 1993): 6.

_____. "The 'Boom' Boom." 15, no. 10 (October, 1993): 6.

Anand, Vineeta. "Baby Boomers to Retire Better Than Parents." *Pensions & Investments.* 37 (September, 1993): 1.

Anderson, P., A. Gustman, and Y. Steinmeier. "Research Grant Summary: Trends in Labor Force Participation and Retirement: A Non-technical Summary of a Final Report to the Social Security Administration, September, 1994." *Social Security Bulletin,* 57, no. 4 (Winter, 1994): 55–58.

Andrews, Emily, and Deborah J. Chollet. "Future Sources of Retirement Income: Whither the Baby Boom." In *Social Security and Private Pensions.*

Ed. Susan Wacheter. Lexington, MA: Lexington Books, 1988.

Anzick, Michael. "Demographic and Employment Shifts: Implications for Benefits and Economic Security." *Employee Benefit Research Institute Brief.* 140 (1993): 1–22.

Appelbaum, Eileen. *The New American Workplace: Transforming Work Systems in the United States.* Ithaca, NY: ILR Press, 1994.

Appelbaum, Eileen, and Ronald Schettkat, eds. *Labor Market Adjustments to Structural Change and Technological Progress.* New York: Praeger, 1990.

Atchley, Robert C. *Social Forces and Aging.* Belmont, CA: Wadsworth Publishing, 1988.

_____. "The Process of Retirement: Comparing Men and Women." In *Women's Retirement: Policy Implications of Recent Research.* Ed. M. Szinovacz. Beverly Hills, CA: Sage Publications, 1982.

Barnes, Carla, B.A. Given, and C. W. Given. "Parent Caregivers: A Comparison of Employed and Not Employed Daughters." *Social Work.* 40, no. 3 (May, 1995): 375–381.

Barth, Michael C. and William McNaught. "The Impact of Future Demographic Shifts on the Employment of Older Workers." *Human Resource Management,* 30, no. 1 (Spring, 1991): 31–44.

Bean, Frank D. "The Baby Boom and Its Explanations." *Sociological Quarterly,* 24 (Summer, 1983): 357.

Beehr, T.A. "The Process of Retirement: A Review and Recommendations for Future Investigation." *Personnel Psychology.* 39 (Spring, 1986): 31–55.

Belgrave, Linda L. "Understanding Women's Retirement." *Generations.* 13 (Spring, 1989): 49–52.

Bernheim, B. Douglas. "At Issue: Will Baby Boomers Be as Well-Off in Retirement as Their Parents?" *CQ Researcher.* 3, no. 41 (November 5, 1993): 977.

_____. *Is the Baby Boom Generation Preparing Adequately for Retirement? Summary Report.* New York: Merrill Lynch, 1993.

Birren, J., P. Robinson, and J. Livingston. *Age, Health and Employment.* Englewood Cliffs, NJ: Prentice-Hall, Inc., 1986.

Bluestone, Irving. *Negotiating the Future: A Labor Perspective on American Business.* New York: Basic Books, 1992.

Bluestone, Irving, and Bennett Harrison. *The Deindustrialization of America.* New York: Basic Books. 1982.

Bluestone, Irving, R.J.V. Montgomery, and John D. Owen, eds. *Aging of the American Workforce: Problems, Programs, Policies.* Detroit, MI: Wayne State University Press, 1990.

Boaz, R.F. "Work as a Response to Low and Decreasing Real Income During Retirement." *Research on Aging.* 9, no. 3 (1987).

Borsch-Supan, Axel. "Population Aging: Social Security Design, and Early Retirement." *Journal of Institutional and Theoretical Economics.* 148, no. 4 (December, 1992): 533–557.

Borzi, Phyllis C. "Women and Their Retirement Income: Will It Be Enough?" *Government Finance Review.* 11, no. 5 (October, 1995): 46–48.

Bouvier, Leon F., and Carol J. DeVita. "Baby Boom—Entering Midlife." *Population Bulletin.* 26, no. 3 (November, 1991): 35.

_____. "America's Baby Boom Generation: The Fateful Bulge." *Population Bulletin.* 35, no. 1 (1980).

Braus, Patricia. "The Baby Boom at Mid-Decade." *American Demographics.* 17, no. 4 (April 1995): 40–45.

Brubaker E., and T. H. Brubaker. "The Context of Retired Women as Caregivers." In *Families and Retirement.* Ed. M. Szinovacz. Newbury Park, CA: Sage Publications, 1992.

Bumpass, L. "What's Happening to the Family? Interactions Between Demographic and Institutional Change." *Demography.* 27, no. 4 (1990): 438–498.

Bureau of Labor Statistics. "Outlook 1990–2005." *Bureau of Labor Statistics Bulletin 2042.* Washington, D.C.: U.S. Department of Labor, May 1992.

Burtless, Gary, and Alicia H. Munnell. "Does a Trend Toward Early Retirement Create Problems for the Economy?" *New England Economic Review.* (November-December, 1990): 17–32.

Calasanti, Toni M. "Gender and Life Satisfaction in Retirement on Assessment of the Male Model." *Journal of Geronotology.* 51, no. 1 (January, 1996): S18–S29.

_____. "Bringing in Diversity: Toward an Inclusive Theory of Retirement." *Journal of Aging Studies.* 7, no. 2 (Summer, 1993): 133–150.

Calasanti, Toni M., and A. Bonanno. "Theorizing About Gender and Aging: Beginning with the Voices of Women." *The Gerontologist.* 32, no. 2 (1992): 280–282.

_____. "Working Over-Time: Economic Restructuring and Retirement of a Class." *The Sociological Quarterly.* 33, no. 1 (1992): 135–152.

Campione, Wendy A. "The Married Women's Retirement Decision: A Methodological Comparison." *Journal of Gerontology.* 42 (July, 1987): 381–386.

Cantor, Richard, and Andrew Yuengert. "The Baby Boom Generation and Aggressive Savings." *Federal Reserve Bank of New York Quarterly Review.* 19, no. 2 (Summer/Fall 1994): 76–91.

Cappo, Joe. "Planning for Older America." *Future Scope: Success Strategies for the 1990s and Beyond.* Chicago, IL: Longman Financial Services Publications, 1990.

Clark, Robert. "Population Aging and Work Rates of Older Persons: An International Comparison." In *As the Workforce Ages.* Ed. Oliva S. Mitchell. Ithaca, NY: ILR Press, 1993.

Clark, Robert, and Richard Anker. "Labour Force Participation Rates of Older Persons: An International Comparison." *International Labor Review.* 129, no. 2 (1990): 255–271.

Clark, Robert, Juanita Kreps, and Joseph Spengler. "Economics of Aging: A Survey." *Journal of Economic Literature.* 26 (September, 1978): 919–962.

Clark, Robert, and Ann A. McDermed. "Determinants of Retirement by Married Women." *Social Security Bulletin.* 52, no. 1 (January, 1989): 33–36.

Coates, Joseph F., Jennifer Jarratt, and John B. Mahaffie. *Future Work: Seven Critical Forces Reshaping Work and the Work Force in North America.* San Francisco, CA: Jossey-Bass, 1990.

Cole, Gerald, and Marjorie N. Taylor. "Caught Between Demographics and the Deficit: How Can Retirement Plans Meet the Challenges Ahead?" *Compensation & Benefits Review.* 28, no. 1 (Jan/Feb, 1996): 32–39.

Comman, John M., and Eric R. Kingson. "Trends, Issues, Perspectives, and Values for the Aging of the Baby Boom Cohorts." *The Gerontologist.* 36, no. 1 (1996): 15–26.

Cooper, Mary H. "Paying for Retirement." *Congressional Quarterly.* 3, no. 41 (November 5, 1993).

Coulson, L. Ann. "Labor Market Participation and Earnings by Female Members of the Baby Boom Generation." *Home Economics Research Journal.* 22, no. 4 (June, 1994): 441–459.

Crooks, Louise. "Women and Pensions: Inequities for Older Women." *Vital Speeches.* (February 15, 1991): 283–285.

Crown, William H., Phyllis H. Mutschler, James H. Schulz, and Rebecca Loew. *Economic Status of Divorced Older Women.* Policy Center on Aging, Heller School, Brandeis University, 1993.

Crystal, Stephen. "Work and Retirement in the Twenty-First Century." *Generations.* 12, no. 3 (Spring, 1988): 60–64.

Crystal, Stephen, Dennis Shea, and Shreeram Krishnaswami. "Educational Attainment, Occupational History, and Stratification: Determinants of Later-Life Economic Outcomes." *Journal of Gerontology.* 47 (September, 1992): S213–221.

Cullison, William E. "The Changing Labor Force: Some Provocative Findings." *Economic Review.* 75, no. 5 (Sept/Oct, 1989): 30–36.

Cutler, Neal E., and Steven J. Devlin. "A Report Card on the Baby Boom's Retirement Planning Efforts." *Journal of the American Society of CLU & ChFC.* 50, no. 1 (January, 1996): 30–32.

_____. "Expansion of the Prime-Lifers: Early Baby Boom Retirement and Early Financial Planning. *Journal of the American Society of CLU & ChFC.* 45, no. 4 (July, 1991): 24–27.

Dennis, H., and H. Axel. *Encouraging Employee Self-Management in Financial and Career Planning.* New York, NY: The Conference Board, 1991.

Dent, Harry, Jr. *Job Shock: Four New Principles Transforming Our Work and Business.* New York: St. Martin's Press, 1995.

Devine, Theresa J. "Characteristics of Self-Employed Women in the United States." *Monthly Labor Review.* 117, no. 3 (March, 1994): 20–34.

DeViney, Stanley. "Life Course, Private Pension, and Financial Well-Being." *American Behavioral Scientist.* 39, no. 2 (Nov/Dec, 1995): 172–185.

Dex, Shirley. *Women's Occupational Mobility: A Lifetime Perspective.* New York: St. Martin's Press. 1987.

Dimeo, Jean. "Women Receive the Short End When It Comes to Their Retirement Pension Incomes." *Pension World.* 28 (October, 1992): 28.

Doeringer, Peter B., ed. *Bridges to Retirement.* Ithaca, New York: Cornell

University, 1990.

Doress-Worters, Paula B. "Adding Elder Care to Women's Multiple Roles: A Critical Review of the Caregiver Stress and Multiple Roles Literatures." *Sex Roles.* 31, no. 9/10 (1994): 597–616.

Dortch, Shannon. "A Slow Fade for the Echo Boom." *American Demographics.* 16, no. 7 (July, 1994): 15–16.

Durgin, Hillary. "Early Retirement Options Likely." *Pensions & Investments.* 18, no. 2 (October 1, 1990): 2.

Easterlin, Richard A. "The Economic Impact of Prospective Population Changes in Advanced Industrial Countries: An Historical Perspective." *Journal of Gerontology.* 46, no. 6 (1991): S299–309.

_____. *Birth and Fortune: The Impact of Numbers on Personal Welfare.* Chicago, IL: University of Chicago Press, 1987.

Easterlin, Richard A., C. MacDonald, and D. Macunovich. "Retirement Prospects of the Baby Boom Generation: A Different Perspective." *The Gerontologist.* 30, no. 6 (1990): 776–783.

Easterlin, Richard A., Christine M. Schaeffer, and Diane J. Macunovich. "Will the Baby Boomers Be Less Well Off Than Their Parents? Income, Wealth, and Family Circumstances Over the Life Cycle in the United States." *Population & Development Review.* 19, no. 3 (September, 1993): 497–522.

Edwards, Richard C., Michael Reich, and David M. Gordon, eds. *Labor Market Segmentation.* Lexington, MA: D.C. Heath, 1975.

Eitzen, D. Stanley, and Maxine B. Zinn, eds. *The Reshaping of America: Social Consequences of the Changing Economy.* Englewood Cliffs, NJ: Prentice-Hall, 1989.

Ekerdt, David J., and Stanley DeViney. "On Defining Persons as Retired." *Journal of Aging Studies.* 4, no. 3 (1990): 211–229.

Employee Benefit Research Institute (EBRI). "Demographic and Employment Shifts: Implications for Benefits and Economic Society." *EBRI Issue Brief Number 140* (August, 1993): 22.

Erdner, Ruth Ann, and Rebecca F. Guy. "Career Identification and Women's Attitudes Toward Retirement." *International Journal of Aging and Human Development.* 30, no. 2 (1990): 129–139.

Ettner, Susan L. "The Impact of 'Parent Care' on Female Labor Supply Decisions." *Demography.* 132, no. 1 (February, 1995): 63–80.

Even, William E., and David A. Macpherson. "Gender Differences in Pensions." *Journal of Human Resources.* 29, no. 2 (Spring, 1994): 555–587.

Feldstein, Martin. "The Missing Piece in Policy Analysis: Social Security Reform." *American Economic Review.* 86, no. 2 (May, 1996): 1–14.

Felmlee, Diane H. "Causes and Consequences of Women's Employment Discontinuity, 1967–1973." *Work and Occupations.* 22, no. 2 (May, 1995): 167–187.

Ferber, Marianne A. "Women's Employment and the Social Security System." *Social Security Bulletin.* 56, no. 3 (Fall, 1993): 33–55.

Feuerbach, Eileen J., and Carol J. Erdwins. "Women's Retirement: The Influence of Work History." *Journal of Women and Aging.* 6, no. 3 (1994): 69–85.

Fox, Judith H. "Effects of Retirement and Former Work Life on Women's Adaptation in Old Age." *Journal of Gerontology.* 32, no. 2 (1977): 196–202.

Fox, Mary Frank, and Sharlene Hesse-Biber. *Women at Work.* Palo Alto, CA: Mayfield Publishing Company, 1984.

Fullerton, Howard N. "Labor Force Change Exaggerated." *Population Today.* 21, no. 5 (May, 1993): 6–9.

_____. "Another Look at the Labor Force." *Monthly Labor Review.* 116, no. 11 (November, 1993): 31–40.

_____. "Labor Force Projections: The Baby Boom Moves On." *Monthly Labor Review.* 114, no. 11 (November, 1991): 31–44.

Gendell, Murray, and Jacob S. Siegal, "Trends in Retirement Age by Sex, 1950–2005." *Monthly Labor Review.* 115, no. 7 (July, 1992): 22–29.

Gerber, Jerry, Janet Wolff, Walter Klores, and Gene Brown. *Lifetrends: The Future of Baby Boomers and Other Aging Americans.* New York: Macmillan Publishing Company, 1989.

Gibson, Campbell. "The Four Baby Booms." *American Demographics.* 15, no. 11 (November, 1993): 36–40.

Gigy, Lynn L. "Preretired and Retired Women's Attitudes Toward Retirement." *International Journal of Aging and Human Development.* 22, no. 1 (1985/1986): 31–44.

Ginn, Jay. "No Jam Tomorrow: Why Women Are Disadvantaged in Occupational Positions." In *Researching Social Life.* Ed. Gilbert G. Nigel. Newbury Park, CA: Sage Publications, 1993.

Glenn, Norval D. "Rethinking Family Change." *IPA Review.* 47, no. 4 (1995): 17–21.

Goldelier, Maurice. *Rationality and Irrationality in Economics.* London: New Left Books, 1972.

Gordon, David M., Richard Edwards, and Michael Reich. *Segmented Work, Divided Workers.* New York: Cambridge University Press, 1982.

Graebner, William. *A History of Retirement: The Meaning and Function of an American Institution.* New Haven, CT: Yale University Press, 1980.

Gratton, B., and M. R. Haug. "Decision and Adaptation: Research on Female Retirement." *Research on Aging.* 5, no. 1 (1983): 59–76.

Greenwald, Mathew. "Bad News for the Baby Boom." *American Demographics.* 11, no. 2 (February, 1989): 34–37.

Gustman, Alan L., Olivia S. Mitchell, and Thomas L. Steinmeier. "Retirement Measures in the Health and Retirement Study." *Journal of Human Resources.* 30 (*Health and Retirement Study Supplement*) (1995): S57–S83.

_____. "The Role in the Labor Market: A Survey of the Literature." *Industrial & Labor Relations Review.* 47, no. 3 (April 1994): 417–438.

Gustman, Alan L., and Thomas L. Steinmeier, "Retirement in a Family Context: A Structural Model for Husbands and Wives." *NBER Working Paper No. 4629.* National Bureau of Economic Research (January, 1994).

_____. "Pension Portability and Labor Mobility: Evidence from the Survey of Income and Program Participation." *Journal of Public Economics.* 50, no. 3 (March, 1993): 299–323.

_____. "The Stampede Toward Defined Contribution Pension Plans: Fact or Fiction?" *Industrial Relations.* 31, no. 2 (Spring, 1992): 361–369.

Hakim, Catherine. "Five Feminist Myths About Women's Employment." *British Journal of Sociology.* 46, no. 3 (September, 1995): 429–455.

Hannon, Kerry. "Why the Rules Are Different for Women." *Working Women.* 20, no. 8 (September, 1995): 20–24, 78.

Hatch, Laurie R., W. R. Grady, and S. D. McLaughlin. "The Retirement Process Among Older Women in the United States: Changes in the 1970s." *Research on Aging.* 10 (September, 1988): 358–382.

Hatch, Laurie R., and Aaron Thompson. "Family Responsibilities and Women's Retirement." In *Families and Retirement.* Ed. Maximiliane Szinovacz, David Ekerdt and Barbara Vinick. Newbury Park, CA: Sage Publications, 1992.

_____. "Gender Differences in Orientation Toward Retirement from Paid Labor." *Gender & Society.* 6, no. 1 (March, 1992): 66–85.

_____. "Effects of Work and Family on Women's Later-Life Resources." *Research on Aging.* 12, no. 3 (September, 1990): 311–338.

Hayes, Christopher, and Marcie Parker. "Overview of the Literature on Pre-Retirement Planning for Women." *Women in Mid-Life: Planning for Tomorrow.* New York: The Haworth Press, Inc., 1993.

_____. "Women & Retirement: The Harsh Realities." *Best's Review.* 92 (July, 1991): 71–72.

Hayghe, Howard V. "Are Women Leaving the Labor Force?" *Monthly Labor Review.* 117, no. 7 (July, 1994): 37–39.

Hayghe, Howard V., and Suzanne M. Bianchi. "Married Mothers' Work Patterns: The Job-Family Compromise." *Monthly Labor Review.* 117, no. 6 (June, 1994): 24–30.

Hayward, Mark D., and W. R. Grady. "Work and Retirement Among a Cohort of Older Men in the United States, 1966–1983." *Demography.* 27, no. 3 (August, 1990): 337–356.

Hayward, Mark D., and M. C. Liu. "Men and Women in Their Retirement Years: A Demographic Profile." In *Families and Retirement.* Ed. M. Szinovacz. Newbury Park, CA: Sage Publications, 1992.

Henretta, John C. "Gender Differences in Employment After Spouse's Retirement." *Research on Aging.* 15 (June, 1993): 148–169.

Hess, Beth B. "Beyond Dichotomy: Drawing Distinctions and Embracing Differences." *Sociological Forum.* 5, no. 1 (1990): 75–92.

Holden, Karen C., Richard V. Burkhauser, and Daniel J. Feaster. "The Timing of Falls into Poverty After Retirement and Widowhood." *Demography.* 25, no. 3 (August, 1988): 405–414.

Holden, Karen C., and Timothy M. Smeeding. "The Poor, the Rich, and the Insecure Elderly Caught in Between." *Milbank Quarterly.* 68, no. 2 (1990): 191–219.

Honig, Marjorie. "Racial and Ethnic Differences in Women's Labor Force Experience and Retirement Expectations." *Health and Retirement Survey Early Results Workshop.* Institute for Social Research, University of Michigan. 1993.

Hurd, Michael. "The Joint Retirement Decision of Husbands and Wives." *Social*

Security Bulletin. 52 (January, 1989): 29–32.

Iams, Howard. "The 1993 SIPP and CPS Pension Surveys." *Social Security Bulletin.* 58, no. 4 (Winter, 1995): 125–130.

Iams, Howard, and Steven H. Sandell. "Changing Social Security Benefits to Reflect Child-Care Years: A Policy Proposal Whose Time Has Passed." *Social Security Bulletin.* 57, no. 4 (Winter, 1994): 10–24.

IRS Employment Review. "Childcare and Caring Responsibilities Have Significant Impact on Women." No. 579 (March, 1995): 4.

Jacobsen, Joyce P., and Laurence M. Levin. "Effects of Intermittent Labor Force Attachment on Women's Earnings." *Monthly Labor Review.* (September, 1995): 14–19.

Jacobsen, Linda, and Brad Edmondson. "Father Figures." *American Demographics.* 15, no. 8 (August, 1993): 22–27.

Jones, Allen N. "Financial Planning a Necessity for Women." *Manage.* 47, no. 2/3 (February, 1996): 4–5.

Jones, Landon Y. *Great Expectations: America and the Baby Boom Generation.* New York: Coward, McCann and Geoghegan, 1980.

Karpel, Craig. *The Retirement Myth.* New York: Harper Collins Publishers, 1995.

Kathne, Hilda, and Janet Zollinger Giele. *Women's Work and Women's Lives: The Continuing Struggle Worldwide.* Boulder, CO: Westview Press, 1992.

Kilty, K. M. and J. H. Behling. "Retirement Financial Planning Among Professional Workers." *The Gerontologist.* 26, no. 5 (1992): 525–530.

King, Mary C. "Occupational Segregation by Race and Sex." *Monthly Labor Review.* 115, no. 4 (April, 1992): 30–37.

Kingson, Eric R. *Diversity of the Baby Boom Generation: Implications for Their Retirement Years.* American Association of Retired Persons, Forecasting and Environmental Scanning Department, Washington, D.C., April, 1992, 76 p.

_____. "Greying of the Baby Boom in the United States: Framing the Policy Debate." *International Social Security Review.* 44, no. 102 (1991): 5–26.

Kingson, Eric R., and Regina O'Grady-LeShane. "The Effects of Caregiving on Women's Social Security Benefits." *The Gerontologist.* 26, no. 5 (1992): 525–530.

Korczyk, S.M. *Pension Portability Issues Affecting Women.* Washington, D.C.: U.S. Department of Labor, Pension and Welfare Benefits Administration. 1990.

Kramer, Betty J., and Stuart Kipnis. "Eldercare and Work-Role Conflict: Toward an Understanding of Gender Differences in Caregiver Burden." *The Gerontologist.* 35, no. 3 (1995): 340–348.

Krysty, Kaycee W. "It Takes More to Tame the Baby Boomer Beast." *Best's Review.* (March, 1995): 80–85.

Kutscher, Ronald E. "Historical Trends: 1950–92, and Current Uncertainties." *Monthly Labor Review.* 116, no. 11 (November, 1993): 3–10.

Landstrom, Beverly G., and Thomas B. Bainbridge. "What's New in Pensions: Defined Lump Sum Plans." *Compensation & Benefits Review.* 28, no. 1 (January 1, 1996): 40–50.

Lappel, Karen, and Suzanne H. Clain. "Determinants of Voluntary and

Involuntary Part-Time Employment." *Eastern Economic Journal.* 19, no. 1 (Winter, 1993): 59–70.

Lee, Ronald D. "The Formal Demography of Population Aging, Transfers, and the Economic Life Cycle." In *Demography of Aging.* Ed. Linda G. Martin and Samuel H. Preston. Washington, D.C.: National Academy Press, 1994.

Leonard, Frances. *Money and the Mature Woman.* Reading, MA: Addison-Wesley Publishing Company. 1993.

Leonesio, Michael V. "Social Security and Older Workers." In *As the Workforce Ages.* Ed. O. Mitchell. Ithaca, NY: ILR Press, 1993.

Levine, Phillip B., and Olivia S. Mitchell. "Expected Changes in the Workforce and Implications for Labor Markets." In *Demography and Retirement: The Twenty-First Century.* Ed. Anna M. Rappaport and Sylvester J. Schieber. Westport, CT: Praeger, 1993.

Lewenhak, Sheila. *Women and Work: An Historical Survey.* New York: St. Martin's Press, 1980.

Light, Paul. *Baby Boomers.* New York: W. W. Norton, 1988.

Limbacher, Patricia B. "Sending the Message Out." *Pensions & Investments.* 23, no. 14 (September 4, 1995): 10.

Lingg, Barbara A. "Women Beneficiaries Aged 62 or Older, 1960-88." *Social Security Bulletin.* 53, no. 7 (July, 1990): 2–12.

Logue, Barbara J. "Women at Risk: Predictors of Financial Stress for Retired Women Workers." *The Gerontologist.* 31, no. 5 (October, 1991): 657–665.

Loprest, Pamela, Kalman Rupp, and Steven H. Sandell. "Gender, Disabilities, and Employment in the Health and Retirement Study." *Journal of Human Resources 1995.* 30 (Health and Retirement Study Supplement): S293–S318.

Macpherson, David A., and Barry T. Hirsch. "Wages and Gender Composition: Why Do Women's Jobs Pay Less?" *Journal of Labor Economics.* 13, no. 3 (July, 1995): 426–471.

Manchester, Joyce. *Baby Boomers in Retirement: An Early Perspective.* Washington, D.C.: United States Congressional Budget Office. 1993.

McBride, Timothy D. *Women's Retirement Behavior: Implications for Future Policy.* Washington, D.C.: Urban Institute, 1988.

Mergenhagen, Paula, and Patricia Braus. "Rethinking Retirement." *American Demographics.* 16, no. 6 (June, 1944): 28–34.

Merrill Lynch. "Rude Awakening from the American Dream." Princeton, NJ: 4th Annual Merrill Lynch Retirement Planning Survey, 1992.

Miletich, John J. *Retirement: An Annotated Bibliography.* Westport, CT: Greenwood Press, 1986.

Mitchell, Olivia S., Ed. *As the Workforce Ages: Costs, Benefits & Policy Challenges.* Ithaca, NY: ILR Press, 1993.

Moen, Jon R. "Past and Current Trends in Retirement: American Men from 1860–1980." *Economic Review.* 73, no. 4 (July/August, 1988): 16–27.

Moen, Phyllis. "Continuities and Discontinuities in Women's Labor Force Activity." In *Life Course Dynamics.* Ed. Glen H. Elder, Jr. Ithaca, NY: Cornell University Press, 1985.

Montgomery, Mark, and James Cosgrove. "Are Part-Time Women Paid Less?

A Model with Firm-Specific Effects." *Economic Inquiry.* 33, no. 1 (January, 1995): 119–133.

Monthly Labor Review. "Women in Their Forties." 116, no. 6 (June, 1993): 2.
_____. "Labor Month in Review." 115, no. 4 (April, 1992): 2.
_____. "Current Labor Statistics." 114, no. 1 (January, 1991): 69–120.

Moore, Michael. "Merrill Study: Baby Boomers Fail to Feather Retirement Nest." *American Banker.* 158, no. 22 (February 3, 1993): 9.

Morris, Robert, and Scott A. Bass, eds. *Retirement Reconsidered.* New York: Springer Publishing Company, 1988.

Morrison, Malcolm. *The Economics of Aging: The Future of Retirement.* New York: Van Nostrand Reinhold, 1982.

Moss, Anne E. *Women, Pensions and Divorce: Small Reforms That Could Make a Big Difference.* Washington, D.C.: AARP Special Activities Department, Women's Initiative, 1993.

Mui, Ada C. "Caring for Frail Elderly Parents: A Comparison of Adult Sons and Daughters." *The Gerontologist.* 35, no. 1 (1995): 86–93.

National Academy on Aging. *Old Age in the 21st Century: A Report to the Assistant Secretary for Aging.* Washington, D.C.: U.S. Department of Health and Human Services, 1993.
_____. *Survey Sketches New Portrait of Aging America.* Washington, D.C.: U.S. Department of Health and Human Services, 1993.

Newman, Katherine. *Falling from Grace: The Experience of Downward Mobility in the American Middle Class.* New York: Vintage Books, 1988.

O'Grady-Leshane, Regina A., Eric R. Kingson, and June Hoops. *Women and Social Security: An Analysis of the Economic Impact of Late-Life Caregiving-Final Report.* Chestnut Hill, MA: Boston College, Graduate School of Social Work, 1988.

Older Women's League. *The Path to Poverty: An Analysis of Women's Retirement Income.* Mother's Day Report. Washington, D.C.: 1995. Pamphlet.
_____. *Heading for Hardship: Retirement Income for American Women in the Next Century.* Mother's Day Report. Washington, D.C.: 1990. Pamphlet.

O'Neil, Barbara M. "Baby-Boom Economics: Financial Planning for 'The Big Chill' Generation." *Journal of Financial Planning.* 4, no. 3 (July, 1991): 142–146.

O'Reilly, Brian. "Busted Boomers: Here's the Wake Up Call." *Fortune.* 132, no. 2 (July 24, 1995): 52–56.

Oriol, William. "In a Turbulent Economy, the U.S. Work Force is Aging." *Perspective on Aging.* 20, no. 2 (March/April, 1991): 4–8.

Palmore, Erdman B., et al. *Retirement: Causes and Consequences.* New York: Springer, 1985.

Pampel, Fred C. "Life Course: Stages and Institutions: Time for Retirement." *Contemporary Sociology.* 22, no. 1 (January, 1993): 93–94.
_____. "Relative Cohort Size and Fertility: The Socio-Political Context of the Easterlin Effect." *American Sociological Review.* 58 (August, 1993): 496–514.

Parsons, Donald O. "Male Retirement Behavior in the U.S. 1930-1950." *Journal of Economic History.* 51 (September, 1991): 657–674.

Patterson, Martha Priddy. "Women's Employment Patterns and Pension Coverage." Unpublished paper. Washington, D.C.: KPMG Peat Marwick, 1995.

Perkins, Kathleen. "Working-Class Women and Retirement." *Journal of Gerontological Social Work.* 20, no. 3-4 (1993): 129–146.

_____. "Psychosocial Implications of Women and Retirement." *Social Work.* 37 (November, 1992): 526–532.

Peterson, Janice. "Public Policy and the Economic Status of Women in the United States." *Journal of Economic Issues.* 26 (June, 1992): 441–448.

Pfeffer, J. "Some Consequences of Organizational Demography: Potential Impacts of an Aging Work Force on Formal Organizations." In *Aging: Social Change.* Ed. S. Kiesler, J. Morgan, and V. Oppenheimer. New York: Academic Press, 1981.

Piacentini, J. S. "Pension Coverage and Benefit Entitlement: New Findings From 1988." *Employee Benefit Research Institute Brief 94.* Washington, D.C.: EBRI, 1989.

Pienta, Amy M., Jeffrey A. Burr, and Jan E. Mutchler. "Women's Labor Force Participation in Later Life: The Effects of Early Work and Family Experiences." *Journal of Gerontology.* 49, no. 5 (1994): S231–S239.

Pozzebon, S. and O. S. Mitchell. "Married Women's Retirement Behavior." *Journal of Population Economics.* 2, no. 1 (March, 1989): 39–53.

Presser, Harriet B. "Job, Family and Gender: Determinants of Nonstandard Work Schedules Among Employed Americans in 1991." *Demography.* 32, no. 4 (November, 1995): 577–587.

Preston, Samuel. "Demographic Change in the United States, 1970–2050." In *Demography and Retirement: The Twenty-first Century.* Ed. Anna M. Rappaport and Sylvester J. Schieber. Westport, CT: Praeger, 1993.

Quinn, Joseph F., and Richard V. Burkhauser. "Public Policy and the Plans and Preferences of Older Americans." *Journal of Aging & Social Policy.* 6, no. 3 (1994): 5–20.

_____. "Retirement and Labor Force Behavior of the Elderly." In *Demography of Aging.* Ed. Linda G. Martin, and Samuel H. Preston. Washington, D.C.: National Academy Press, 1994.

_____. "Work and Retirement." In *Handbook of Aging and the Social Sciences.* Ed. B. H. Binstock, and L. K. George. New York: Academic Press, 1990.

Rappaport, Anna M. "The Evolving Social Contract and the Role of Retiree Health in the Retirement Package." *Compensation and Benefits Management.* 11, no. 3 (February 2, 1995): 83–86.

Rappaport, Anna M., and Sylvester J. Schieber, eds. *Demography and Retirement: The Twenty-first Century.* Westport, CT: Praeger, 1993.

Rayman, Paula, Kimberly Allshouse and Jessie Allen. "Resiliency Amidst Inequity: Older Women in An Aging United States." In *Women on the Front*

Lines: Meeting the Challenge of an Aging America. Ed. Jessie Allen, and Alan Pifer. Washington, D.C.: Urban Institute Press, 1993.

Reimers, Cordelia, and Marjorie Honig. *Responses to Social Security by Men and Women: Myopic and Far-Sighted Behavior.* Working Paper. Hunter College, October 1993.

Reynolds, Michael J. "Will You be Able to Afford to Retire?" *Savings & Community Banker.* 4, no. 1 (January, 1995): 33–36.

Ricardo-Campbell, Rita, and Edward P. Lazear, eds. *Issues in Contemporary Retirement.* Stanford, CA: Hoover Institution Press, 1988.

Riche, Martha Farnsworth. "Demographic Change and the Destiny of the Working-Age Population." In *As the Workforce Ages.* Ed. Olivia S. Mitchell. Ithaca, NY: ILR Press, 1993.

Rifkin, Jeremy. *The End of Work: The Decline of the Global Labor Force and the Dawn of the Post-Market Era.* New York: G. P. Putnam's Sons, 1995.

Rix, Sara E. "Women and Well-Being in Retirement: What Role for Public Policy?" In *Women in Mid-Life: Planning for Tomorrow.* New York: The Haworth Press, Inc., 1993.

Robison, Julie, Phyllis Moen, and Donna Dempster-McClain. "Women's Caregiving: Changing Profiles and Pathways." *Journal of Gerontology.* 50B, no. 6 (1995): S362–S373.

Ross, Jane L., and Melinda M. Upp. "Treatment of Women in the U.S. Social Security System, 1970–88." *Social Security Bulletin.* 56, no. 3 (Fall, 1993): 56–67.

Russell, Cheryl. "Boomer Nest Eggs." *American Demographics.* 17, no. 7 (July, 1995): 8, 59.

_____. *The Master Trend: How the Baby Boom Generation Is Remaking America.* New York: Plenum Press, 1993.

_____. *100 Predictions for the Baby Boom: The Next 50 Years.* New York: Plenum Press, 1987.

Russell, Louise. *The Baby Boom Generation and the Economy.* Washington, D.C.: Brookings Institution, 1982.

Salisbury, Dallas L. "The Future Role of Pensions in Savings and Retirement Income." *EBRI Notes.* 14, no. 1 (March, 1995): 1–3.

Sandell, Steven H., and Howard Iams. "Caregiving and Women's Social Security Benefits: A Common on Kingson and O'Grady-LeShane." *The Gerontologist.* 34, no. 5 (1994): 680–684.

Schenck-Yglesias, C. G. "A Frail Mom Is a Full-Time Job." *American Demographics.* 17, no. 9 (September, 1995): 14–15.

Schieber, Sylvester J., and John B. Shoven. "Social Security Reform: Around the World in 80 Ways." *American Economic Review.* 86, no. 2 (May 1, 1996): 373–377.

Schulz, James H. *The Economics of Aging.* New York: Auburn House, 1992.

Shack-Marquez, Janice. "Earnings Differences Between Men and Women." *Monthly Labor Review.* 107 (1986): 15–16.

Shank, Susan E. "Women and the Labor Market: The Link Grows Stronger." *Monthly Labor Review.* 111, no. 3 (March, 1988): 3–8.

Shapiro, Harvey D. "The Coming Inheritance Bonanza." *Institutional Investor.* 28, no. 6 (June, 1994): 143–148.

Shaver, Sheila. "Aging, the Baby Boom, and the Crisis in Retirement Income." *The Gerontologist.* 31 (December, 1991): 841–843.

Shaw, Lois B. *Midlife Women at Work: A Fifteen Year Perspective.* Lexington, MA: Lexington Books, 1986.

Skirboll, Esther, and Myrna Silverman. "Women's Retirement: A Case Study Approach." *Journal of Women & Aging.* 4, no. 1 (1992): 77–89.

Slevin, K. F., and C. R. Wingrove. "Women in Retirement: A Review and Critique of Empirical Research Since 1976." *Sociological Inquiry.* 65, no. 1 (February, 1995): 1–21.

Social Security Bulletin. "Income Change at Retirement." 53, no. 1 (January, 1990): 2–10.

Stromberg, Ann H., and Shirley Harkess, eds. *Women Working.* Mountain View, CA: Mayfield Publishing, 1988.

Szinovacz, Maximiliane. "Women and Retirement." In *Growing Old in America.* Ed. Beth B. Hess and Elizabeth W. Markson. New Brunswick, NJ: Transaction Books, 1991.

_____. "Introduction: Research on Women's Retirement." In *Women's Retirement: Policy Implications of Recent Research.* Ed. Maximiliane Szinovacz. Ann Arbor, MI: Sage Publishers, 1982.

Szinovacz, Maximiliane, David Ekerdt, and Barbara Vinick, eds. *Families and Retirement.* Newbury Park, CA: Sage Publications, 1992.

Szinovacz, Maximiliane, and Christine Washo. "Gender Differences in Exposure to Life Events and Adaptations to Retirement." *The Gerontologist.* 47, no. 4 (1992): S191–S196.

Taeuber, Cynthia M., and Jessie Allen. "Women in Our Aging Society: The Demographic Outlook. In *Women on the Front Lines: Meeting the Challenge of an Aging America.* Ed. Jessie Allen and Alan Pifer. Washington, D.C.: Urban Institute Press, 1993.

Talaga, Jean A., and Terry A. Beehr. "Are There Gender Differences in Predicting Retirement Decisions?" *Journal of Applied Psychology.* 80, no. 1 (February, 1995): 16–28.

United States Congressional Budget Office. *Baby Boomers in Retirement: An Early Perspective.* Washington, D.C.: Government Printing Office, 1993.

United States Department of Commerce. *Statistical Abstract of the United States, 1994.* Washington, D.C.: Bureau of the Census, 1994.

_____. "Marital Status and Living Arrangements: March, 1990." *Current Population Report P-20, no. 450.* Washington, D.C.: Bureau of the Census, 1991.

_____. *Statistical Abstract of the United States, 1990.* Washington, D.C.: Bureau of the Census, 1991.

_____. "Projections of the Population of the United States, by Age, Sex and Race: 1988 to 2080." by Gregory Spencer. *Current Population Reports Series P-25, no. 1018.* Washington, D.C.: Bureau of the Census, 1989.

United States Department of Labor. *Women in the Workforce: An Overview.*
Washington, D.C.: Report 892, July, 1995.

———. *Retirement Benefits of American Workers: New Findings from the
September, 1994 Current Population Survey.* Washington, D.C.: Government
Printing Office, 1995.

———. *Top Ten Ways to Beat the Clock and Prepare for Retirement.*
Washington, D.C.: Government Printing Office, 1995. Pamphlet

———. *1993 Handbook on Women Workers: Trends & Issues.* Washington,
D.C.: Women's Bureau, 1994.

———. Bureau of Labor Statistics, unpublished tabulations from *Current
Population Survey,* 1990.

———. *Older Worker Task Force: Key Policy Issues for the Future: Report of
the Secretary of Labor.* Washington, D.C.: Government Printing Office, 1989.

United States House of Representatives, Select Committee on Aging. *How Well
Do Women Fare Under the Nation's Retirement Policies?* Washington, D.C.:
Government Printing Office, 1992.

United States House Select Committee on Aging. *Retirement Income for Women.*
Hearing Before the Subcommittee on Retirement Income and Employment of
the Select Committee on Aging, House of Representatives, Washington, D.C.:
Government Printing Office, July 2, 1990.

———. *Women in Retirement: Are They Losing Out?* Hearing Before the
Subcommittee on Retirement Income and Employment of the Select Committee
on Aging, House of Representatives, One Hundred First Congress, Second
Session, Washington, D.C.: May 22, 1990.

United States National Center for Health Statistics. *Monthly Vital Statistics
Report.* 39, no. 12, Washington, D.C.: Government Printing Office. [date?]

United States Senate Special Committee on Aging. *Aging America: Trends and
Projections, 1991.* Washington, D.C.: U.S. Government Printing Office.

Urban Institute. *Earnings Sharing in Social Security: A Model for Reform.*
Washington, D.C.: Center for Women Policy Studies, 1988.

Van Horn, Susan Housholder. *Women, Work and Fertility, 1900–1986.* New
York: New York University Press, 1988.

Vitt, Lois A., and Jurg K. Siegenthaler, eds. *Encyclopedia of Financial
Gerontology.* Westport, CT: Greenwood Press, 1996.

Voges, Wolfgang, and Hannelore Pongratz. "Retirement and the Lifestyles of
Older Women." *Ageing and Society.* 8 (March, 1988): 63–83.

Waitley, Denis. *Empires of the Mind: Lessons to Lead and Succeed in a
Knowledge-Based World.* New York: William Morrow and Company, Inc.,
1995.

Waldrop, Judith. "The Baby Boom Turns 45." *American Demographics.* 13, no.
1 (January, 1991): 22–27.

Weaver, David A. "Work and Retirement Decisions of Older Women: A
Literature Review." *Social Security Bulletin.* 57, no. 1 (Spring, 1994): 3–24

Westoff, Charles F. "Some Speculations on the Future of Marriage and Family."
Family Planning Perspectives. 10, no. 2 (March/April, 1978): 80.

Wiatrowski, William J. "Factors Affecting Retirement Income." *Monthly Labor Review.* 116, no. 3 (March, 1993): 25–35.

Wilensky, Harold L. "The Great American Job Creation Machine in Comparative Perspective." *Industrial Relations.* 31, no. 3 (Fall, 1992): 473–487.

Williams, Donald R. "Women's Part-Time Employment: A Gross Flows Analysis." *Monthly Labor Review.* 118, no. 4 (April, 1995): 36–43.

Wingrove, C. Ray, and Kathleen F. Slevin. "Sample of Professional and Managerial Women: Success in Work and Retirement." *Journal of Women and Aging.* 3, no. 2 (1991): 95–117.

Wise, David A., Ed. *Issues in the Economics of Aging.* Chicago: University of Chicago, 1990.

———. *The Economics of Aging.* Chicago: University of Chicago, 1989.

Witkowski, Kristine M., and Kevin T. Leight. "The Effects of Gender Segregation, Labor Force Participation, and Family Roles on the Earnings of Young Adult Workers." *Work and Occupations.* 22, no. 1 (February, 1995): 48–72.

Wood, Robert G., Mary E. Corcoran, and Paul N. Courant. "Pay Differences Among the Highly Paid: The Male-Female Earnings Gap in Lawyers' Salaries." *Journal of Labor Economics.* 11, no. 3 (July, 1993): 417–441.

Woods, John R. "Pension Coverage Among the Baby Boomers: Initial Findings From a 1993 Survey." *Social Security Bulletin.* 57, no. 3 (Fall, 1994): 12–25.

Wyatt, Edward. "For Mutual Funds, New Political Muscle." *New York Times,* September 8, 1996.

Wyatt, Lindsay. "How Proposed Changes Will Affect Private Plans." *Pension Management.* 31, no. 9 (September, 1995): 10–15.

Wysocki, Bernard. "Early Retirement Isn't in the Boomer's Future." *Wall Street Journal,* May 6, 1996, p. 1.

Index

About the Author

NANCY DAILEY, Ph.D., is the co-founder of Dailey & O'Brien, Inc. She has extensive expertise in executive management on issues concerning women, work, and retirement.

ISBN 0-275-96070-6

HARDCOVER BAR CODE